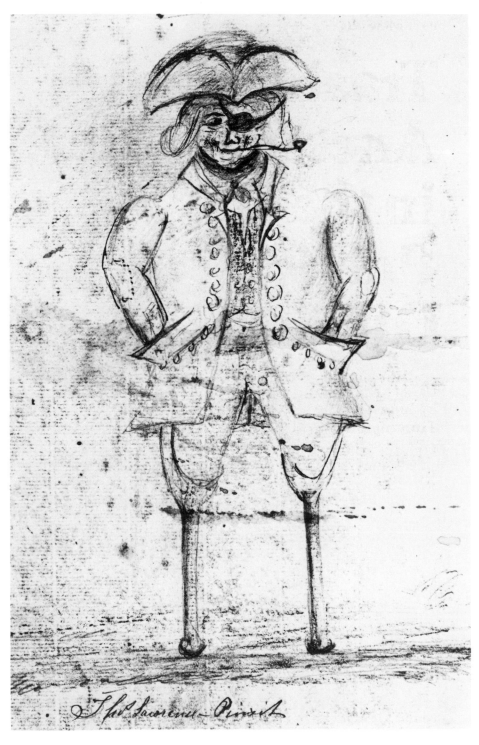

Frontispiece: Sketch in a General Register of Greenwich Hospital Pensioners. Early nineteenth century (ADM 6/322)

Public Record Office Handbooks No 19

Tracing your Ancestors in the Public Record Office

by Jane Cox and
Timothy Padfield

London: Her Majesty's Stationery Office

ISBN 0 11 440186 1

Contents

Abbreviations

MS   Manuscript
PCC   Prerogative Court of Canterbury
PRO   Public Record Office
TS   Typescript

Other letters are Public Record Office codes representing classes of records.

Introduction

The Public Record Office houses one of the finest, most complete archives in Europe, comprising the records of the central government and law courts from Domesday Book to the present century. It is a mine of information for the family historian but it is not the place to begin your research as the main collections of birth, marriage and death records are held elsewhere. There is, moreover, no central index of names, and so the more you can discover about your family in advance the speedier and the more fruitful your researches in the public records will be.

The PRO does not undertake genealogical research but references to specific records may be supplied in some cases if adequate information is given. Photocopies can be ordered by post if the documents are identified by the applicant (explained in PRO Reference Guide no. 19). You will have to come to the search rooms to conduct your own research, unless you are prepared to employ a record agent (see VI below).

The Public Record Office has three repositories:

Modern Departmental records	Public Record Office Ruskin Avenue Kew Richmond Surrey TW9 4DU Telephone 01-876 3444
Medieval and Early Modern records and all legal records	Public Record Office Chancery Lane London WC2A 1LR Telephone 01-405 0741
Census Returns only	Census Room of Public Record Office Land Registry Building Portugal Street London WC2A 3HP Telephone 01-405 3488

If you wish to consult the public records, you should ring the office to ascertain which repository you will need to visit. The search rooms are open to the public from 9.30 a.m. to 5 p.m., Monday to Friday, except on public holidays and during the first two weeks in October. A reader's ticket will be issued to you when you arrive on production of some positive means of identification such as a banker's card. You will not need a ticket if you are intending to consult only census returns.

Records in the Public Record Office must be ordered by their call numbers, comprising group letters (e.g. WO, for War Office), class number (e.g. WO 97, for War Office, Soldiers' Documents) and piece number (e.g. WO 97/341, for War Office, Soldiers' Documents, 13th Foot, Abb-Car, 1760–1854).

The bibliographies in this book contain, besides works for further reading and the names of the relevant record classes, information on various aids to finding and understanding the records. These can be in one of several forms:

a Transcript: a full text, in which the abbreviations of the original manuscripts have been extended wherever this could be done with certainty.

b Calendar: a precis, usually in English, full enough for most purposes to replace the original documents.

c List: an enumeration of the units composing a class of records, with dates and simple descriptions.

d Descriptive list: a list with brief abstracts of documents.

e Index: alphabetically arranged references to people, places or subjects mentioned in the records.

f Catalogue: a calendar or descriptive list containing records of similar content drawn from different groups or classes, sometimes for a special purpose such as a public exhibition.

It must be emphasised, that there is no single finding aid which gives precise references to all the records. Unpublished finding aids are to be found in the PRO unless otherwise stated.

Public records are normally closed for 30 years from the date of their creation, thus a file opened in 1950 and closed in 1955 becomes available in 1986. Exceptions to this rule are noted below.

There is a list of addresses referred to in the text, given at the end.

The section on Deeds and other Records of Land-ownership was written by David Thomas.

Front cover photograph: Clive Friend

I For the beginner: preparation and method

Before searching original records, you must gather together any information that may already be in the family: oral tradition, pedigrees in family bibles, letters, diaries, etc. Always work backwards; it is very difficult to work forwards on the basis of a tradition that says you are descended from a younger brother of Robert the Bruce. The paternal line is normally more easily established than the maternal. There are a number of inexpensive paper-back guides in print which are worth reading before you start. Having acquired the rudiments of genealogy, you will need various works to help you interpret the records (which are often written in a difficult and unfamiliar hand and, before 1733, may be in Latin) and to help you find your way to the records you need.

It is a good idea to make a preliminary investigation to find out whether someone has worked on your family or is currently doing so. The Federation of Family History Societies can help; there are a number of local family history groups and one-name societies in existence and the Federation will supply a list. Enquiries should be addressed to the General Secretary. You can also consult the *National Genealogical Directory* for this purpose. There are numerous pedigrees in print and the library of the Society of Genealogists has a large collection. Many county record offices have card indexes of surnames; these can be very useful if you know roughly where your family came from.

The Federation of Family History Societies and the Society of Genealogists both produce leaflets on starting genealogy and most county record offices published leaflets on their own genealogical holdings.

Books

Guide to the Contents of the Public Record Office (London 1963, 1968)
K A Buckley, *Ancestry Tracing* (Birmingham, 1978)
D Iredale, *Discovering your Family Tree* (Aylesbury, 1977)
A Camp, *Everyone has Roots* (London, 1978)
E A Gooder, *Latin for Local History* (2nd edn., London, 1978)
Handbook of Dates for Students of English History, ed. C R Cheney (London, 1961)
National Genealogical Directory, ed. M J Burchall and J Warren (Brighton, 1979, 1980, 1981)
F G Emmison, *How to read Local Archives, 1500–1700* (London, 1967)
D M Field, *Step-by-Step Guide to Tracing your Ancestors* (London, 1982)

R Harvey, *Genealogy for Librarians* (London, 1983)
C T Martin, *The Record Interpreter* (2nd edn., London, 1910)
R E Latham, *Revised Medieval Latin Word-List* (London, 1965)
M J Kaminkov, *New Bibliography of British Genealogy* (Baltimore, 1965)
J Foster and J Sheppard, *British Archives* (London, 1983)
Record Repositories in Great Britain (London, 1979)
S Grimaldi, *Origines Genealogicae* (London, 1828)
R Sims, *Manual for the Genealogist* (London, 1856)
H B Guppy, *Homes of Family Names in Britain* (Baltimore, 1968)
P H Reaney, *Dictionary of British Surnames* (2nd edn., London, 1976)
C W Bardsley, *Dictionary of English and Welsh Surnames* (London, 1901)
The Surname Book and Racial History, ed. S Y Gates (Salt Lake City, 1918)
E Machysaght, *The Surnames of Ireland* (I.U.P., 1973)
G F Black, *The Surnames of Scotland: their Origin, meaning and history* (N.Y., 1962)
P Laslett, *The World we have lost* (2nd edn., London, 1971)
D Gardner and F Smith, *Genealogical Research in England and Wales* (Utah, 1956)

Unpublished Finding Aids

Index of Interesting and Unusual Christian Names (card index, apply to D Harrington)

Current Guide to the Contents of the Public Record Office. (Some of the earlier groups of records have not yet been included. Microfiche copy can be bought from the PRO.)

II What to use in the Public Record Office

Do not start your search in the Public Record Office. Records of births, marriages and deaths, with some exceptions, are to be found elsewhere (see III/1 below). In general the genealogist has recourse to the public records for the following purposes:

to consult the Census Returns for 1841, 1851, 1861, 1871 and 1881 (see III/2 below);

to trace nonconformist (protestant or Roman Catholic) births, marriages and deaths, before 1837 (see III/1 and IV/13, 14 below);

to trace ancestors who had or might have had some connection with the Crown or the Services (see IV/1-5, 7 below);

to find wills of (usually) wealthy ancestors who lived (usually) in the south of England or abroad, before 1858, and to consult the Death Duty Registers (see III/3 below);

to find eighteenth century London marriages not recorded elsewhere (see III/1 below);

to find mentions of ancestors leaving or entering the country (see IV/15, 17 below);

to trace criminals or bankrupts (see IV/20, 21 below);

to go back beyond the period for which there are parish registers, i.e. before the sixteenth century (see V below).

A glance at the appendix and the list of contents will give you an idea of some of the questions that can be answered in the Public Record Office.

III Some useful groups of records

There are 83 miles of public records and all sorts of information may be found. This handbook deals only with some of the major sources for compiling a family history. For a more detailed description of the Public Record Office's holdings see the published *Guide.* An updated version, the Current Guide, is available on the Reference Room shelves; microfiche copy may be purchased. *British National Archives* gives information about officially published records and printed lists and indexes.

Books

Guide to the Contents of the Public Record Office (London 1963, 1968)
British National Archives (Government Publications Sectional List 24, revised annually)

1 Births, Marriages and Deaths

a After 1837

Civil registration of births, marriages and deaths started in England and Wales in July 1837. The records are not held by the Public Record Office, but by the General Register Office, Office of Population Censuses and Surveys. There are two search rooms: St Catherine's House for births and marriages and Alexandra House for deaths. Correspondence to be directed to the former. Searchers are not permitted to look at the original records, and no information is available except that which is in the form of a copy certificate, which you need to purchase. A copy certificate, which takes 48 hours to prepare, can be applied for in person, if you find the reference in the indexes yourself, or by post, if you give the details of the registration you require. The certificates of births, marriages and deaths are filed separately, and reference to them is by quarterly indexes. The public search room is open from 8.30 a.m. to 4.30 p.m. Monday to Friday.

Failure to find a birth, marriage or death in the indexes may be ascribable to one of the following reasons:

Before 1875 there was no penalty for non-registration and there may be omissions in the birth and death registers; marriages were usually registered as this was done by the officiating clergyman or Registrar.

From 1835 workhouses kept their own birth registers and many births were never registered centrally.

Before 1927 there was no formal adoption procedure and there is no record of the birth of the adopted child under the name by which he was known.

There may have been a clerical error when the entry in the local Registrar's register was transferred to the central registry. It is worth checking the Superintendent Registrar's records which are kept in the district registeries.

Some people were known by a christian name which was not the first forename on their birth certificate.

In the nineteenth century approximately 10% of marriages took place *after* the birth of the first child.

b Before 1837
The prime source for births, marriages and deaths (or rather, baptisms, marriages and burials) from the sixteenth century to 1837 is the parish register. These registers are not kept at the Public Record Office: to locate the whereabouts of one, contact the appropriate county record office, whose address will be in *Record Repositories in Great Britain.* The Society of Genealogists (see VI below) has transcripts of a large number of parish registers, and it is also in the process of publishing a national index of them. The guide to parish registers produced in *Local Population Studies* is useful. The Society also has a large collection of transcripts of monumental inscriptions.

i Non-parochial Registers
The registers kept by nonconformist churches (i.e. those deviating from the Anglican church) are mostly in the Public Record Office (c. 9000 registers), although very many chapel registers have disappeared. Others may be with the congregation or deposited locally. The registers in the PRO are mainly the records of protestant congregations (RG 4–RG 8). There are a few Roman Catholic registers from the north; others remain in the custody of the appropriate priest-in-charge, unless they have been deposited for safe custody with denominational, record or historical societies. Most of these registers are in the Mormon International Genealogical Index (see p. 7 below).

There are other registers in the PRO which may be useful sources, for example those of the British Lying-in Hospital, Holborn, which was established in 1749. It catered for the 'distressed poor (married women only) with special attention to the wives of soldiers and sailors'. There was provision both for in and out care, i.e. assistance was given with home deliveries, though most of the patients were provided with a bed in the hospital. The registers (RG 8/52–66) are in two series and run from 1749 to 1868. The 'Particulars of Patients' give the name of the patient and her husband, her parish of settlement (not her home address), date when the baby was due, date when it arrived, date of the child's baptism, its name and sex, date of the mother's admission and discharge (or death), after 1751 the mother's age and from 1755 the occupation of the father and the 'character' of the labour (normal, breech etc.). After 1812 they started giving the home address of the couple. The registers, with indexes, of the nonconformist burial ground in London, at Bunhill Fields, are also in the PRO (RG 4, RG 8). The Society of Genealogists has an index to the Bunhill Fields Books of Interment, vols. 11–18 (1828–1854) in their Middlesex section; and Interment Order Books, 1789–1854, are at the Guildhall Library, as is an index of persons buried 1827–1838. The registers of the Lying-in Hospital and Bunhill Fields have been included in the Mormon International Genealogical Index. The registers of the former Rolls Chapel are in the PRO (PRO 30/21). The registers of the Bethnal Green Gibraltar Row Burial Ground are a recent deposit.

Although nonconformity started in the mid-sixteenth century, few registers pre-date 1700. Most cover the period 1775–1837. After 1754 nonconformists were obliged to marry in the local parish church so, from this date, there are usually only baptismal registers. This does not apply to Quakers and Jews (who were specifically excluded from the statute), and Roman Catholics (who largely ignored it). Nonconformist baptisms *may* be found in parochial registers of the established church following an act of 1695. Immigrants maintained their own 'foreign' churches.

It should be borne in mind that nonconformist registers often served a far wider area than did the parish church. Clues that may suggest that a search of the nonconformist registers might be fruitful are:

a family tradition;

a post 1837 marriage that took place either in a nonconformist chapel or a register office (this happened if the particular denomination did not have a registered meeting house);

if a parish register has a suspiciously high number of marriages and burials of one surname, in proportion to the number of baptisms.

As relatively few registers survive, if you have been unable to find your nonconformist ancestor, it is a good idea to look at the Court Rolls for the area (see V below). For London nonconformists between 1742 and 1840, the Dr Williams' Library Collection is very useful. There was also a central metropolitan registry for Methodists, 1818–1841. See also IV/13 below, and the Society of Genealogists *National Index*, vol. II.

ii Marriages

Until Lord Hardwicke's Marriage Act (26 Geo. II, c. 33) came into operation in 1754, marriages did not necessarily take place in the local parish church and marriages before this date may be difficult to find. Marriages are, in any case, always difficult to locate, as it was the parish church of the bride which was often chosen for the ceremony. In the eighteenth century it was fashionable to marry by licence for privacy or subterfuge. J S W Gibson's book gives a guide to the whereabouts of marriage licences, allegations (the affidavits sworn by the parties) and bonds, and there is a list of marriage indexes in *The Genealogists' Magazine*. The Boyd marriage index at the Society of Genealogists has a 12% coverage of English marriages from 1538 (see VI below).

In London, before 1754, there were a number of 'marriage shops' for ordinary folk, also patronised by the gentry. Until 1675 the popular place to marry was St James', Duke's Place at Aldgate. From the 1620s to c. 1700 the other 'marriage church' was Holy Trinity, Minories (registers in the Guildhall Library). St Benet's, Paul's Wharf, was also popular, as it was near the Faculty Office. From 1674 until 1754 large numbers of marriages were conducted by irregular clergy in and around the Fleet Prison, and also in Mayfair, in the Mint at Southwark and in the King's Bench Prison, the records of which are in the PRO (RG 7). The Fleet Registers should be treated with extreme caution as the dates given are unreliable, and names, indeed whole entries, may be fictitious. Such clandestine marriages could result in prosecution, and there are the records of many such cases among the *ex officio* Act Books of the Commissary Court of London in the Guildhall Library and the records of the London Consistory Court in the Greater London Record Office. The Pallot Index, covering the years 1742–1837, contains marriages from most established churches in London, and extracts from nonconformist registers. It is held by the Institute of Heraldic and Genealogical Studies (see VII below) who will search it for a fee.

For the whereabouts of records of irregular, border or 'Gretna Green' marriages, see the *Genealogists' Magazine*, vol XX.

iii Divorce

Before 1858 (except in Scotland) divorce was rare and expensive, and achieved by private bill in the House of Lords. There was only one divorce bill before 1670. The church courts could decree a legal separation, known as divorce *a mensa et thoro*, but the parties had to undertake not to remarry. Alternatively the marriage could be dissolved *ab initio* on the grounds of pre-contract, a not uncommon procedure which was abolished in 1754. Records of the proceedings in the church courts, which are deposited in diocesan record offices, are largely unindexed and can be extremely difficult to interpret.

Records of divorce from 1858 to 1934 are in the PRO (J 77, J 78). The files, but not the indexes, are closed for 75 years, although permission to consult individual case papers may be obtained from the Principal Registry of the Family Division at Somerset House. For divorces since 1937, you should also apply to the Family Division.

iv Adoption

Certificates of any adoption in England and Wales since 1 January 1927 may be obtained from the Registrar General. They show the date of the adoption, the name of the child as adopted, and the full name and address of the adoptive parents. For information as to how to obtain a birth certificate, the adopted person should apply to the General Register Office (CA Section). Before 1927 there was no system of legal adoption and it is usually extremely difficult to trace private arrangements.

v Extra Finding Aids for Births and Deaths

One of the most useful genealogical aids now available is the Computer File

Index (CFI) compiled by the Church of Jesus Christ of Latter Day Saints (Mormons). This is now known as the International Genealogical Index (IGI). It is an index mainly of the baptismal entries in a large proportion of the parish registers, and some nonconformist and synagogue registers, in the British Isles. A microfiche copy can be consulted in the PRO, at the Hyde Park Chapel, at some other Mormon chapels, in the Guildhall Library and at the Society of Genealogists (see VI below) where you will need to book a reader. The IGI is widely available in the USA, Australia and New Zealand. Some local record offices hold copies of those parts of the index which relate to their areas.

The records of the clearance of burial grounds, which relate to c. 190 cemeteries and churchyards and are deposited in the PRO (RG 37), may provide lists of the names found on monumental inscriptions. The files vary in value; some are selective, some have names but no dates, some have full transcriptions. There is a topographically arranged list but no index of names.

For births, marriages and deaths abroad and at sea, see IV/16 below.

Bibliography

Books

Abstract of Arrangements respecting Registration of Births, Marriages and Deaths in the UK and the other Countries of the British Commonwealth of Nations, and in the Irish Republic (London, 1952)
'An Aid to English Research', *Family History*, vol. VII, nos. 38/39, n.s. nos. 14/15 (Aug. 1972), p. 54
K A Buckley, *Ancestry Tracing* (Birmingham, 1978)
A J Camp and L W L Edwards, 'The Computer File Index', *The Genealogists' Magazine*, vol. XIX (1978), pp. 162–163
Greater London Cemeteries and Crematoria and their Registers (Society of Genealogists, 1984)
'Marriage Licences, Bonds and Allegations', *Family History*, vol. V, no. 25, n.s. no. 1 (Jan. 1967), pp. 7–32
National Index of Parish Registers, ed. D J Steel for the Society of Genealogists (London, 1976)
'Original Parish Registers', *Local Population Studies* (1974, 1976, 1978)
G S Crighton, 'Irregular Border Marriages', *The Genealogists' Magazine*, vol. XX (1981), pp. 528–532
'Irregular Border Marriages', *The Genealogists' Magazine*, vol. XX (1981), pp. 415–416
J S W Gibson, *Bishops Transcripts and Marriage Licences* (Banbury, 1981)
A List of Parishes in Boyd's Marriage Index (Society of Genealogists, 1974)
M Walcott and J S W Gibson, *Marriage Indexes* (Federation of Family History Societies, 1982)

Published Finding Aids

Index to Local and Personal Acts, 1801–1947 (London, 1949)

Index to the Local and Personal and Private Acts, 1798-1839, ed. T Vardon
    (London, 1840)
List of Non-parochial Registers and Records in the Custody of the Registrar General,
    Main Series (List and Index Society, vol. 42)
The Registers of St Benet's, Paul's Wharf (Harleian Society, Register Section
    1909-1912, which has also published many other London registers)
The Registers of St James's, Duke's Place, ed. Phillimore and Cockayne
    (London, 1900-1902)

Unpublished Finding Aids

Boyd Marriage Index, Society of Genealogists
Bunhill Fields Interment Order Books, 1789-1854, Guildhall Library
Index to Bunhill Fields Books of Interment, 1828-1854, Society of
    Genealogists (Middlesex Section)
Index of Persons buried in Bunhill Fields, 1827-1838, Guildhall Library
Mormon International Genealogical Index, PRO, Society of Genealogists and
    Guildhall Library
An index to the Fleet marriages is in preparation
An index to the Gibraltar Row Burial Ground Registers is in progress

Records

Supreme Court of Judicature
J 77   Divorce Files, 1858-1934
J 78   Indexes to Divorce Files, 1858-1885

Public Record Office
PRO 30/21   Rolls Chapel Register, 1736-1892

General Register Office
RG 4 Registers, Authenticated, 1567-1858 (includes Burial Registers of
    Bunhill Fields RG4/3014-4001, indexed in 4652-4657, 1713-1838; Dr
    Williams' General Register of Nonconformist baptisms, 1742-1837,
    RG 4/4666-4676; and the registers of the Metropolitan Wesleyan
    Registry, 1818-1841, RG 4/4677-4679)
RG 5 Non-parochial Certificates, 1742-1840
RG 6 Registers, Authenticated, Society of Friends, 1613-1841
RG 7 Registers, Unauthenticated, Fleet, etc., 1667-c. 1777
RG 8 Registers, Unauthenticated, Miscellaneous, 1646-1970 (includes
    Registers of Bunhill Fields Burial Ground, RG 8/35-38, 1833-1853;
    of the Victoria Park Cemetery, Hackney, RG 8/42-51, 1853-1876*; of
    the British Lying-in Hospital, Holborn, RG 8/52-66, 1749-1868 and
    of the Bethnal Green Gibraltar Row Burial Ground, RG 8/305-314,
    1793-1826, index in progress)
RG 37 Removal of Graves or Tombstones, 1923-1982

---

*These registers are alphabetically arranged and give ages and exact addresses.

2 Census Returns

The census returns are the most important modern genealogical source in the PRO. The returns of 1841, 1851, 1861, 1871 and 1881 for England and Wales, including the Isle of Man and the Channel Islands (HO 107, RG 9, RG 10, RG 11) are available on microfilm in the Land Registry Building in Portugal Street, just a few minutes walk from the General Register Office. A number of copies of returns are deposited locally, and a complete microfilm copy is held by the Genealogical Society of Utah. Earlier censuses were of numbers, not names; the few lists of names which survive from the 1801–1831 censuses, are given in J S W Gibson's book. The returns are arranged topographically, and it is therefore essential to know at least the approximate address before starting a search. The information they give, from 1851 onwards, is the name, age, sex, marital status, place of birth and occupation of everyone in the house, and their relationship to the head of the household (see plate I). A good way to use the returns is to take an address from a birth certificate which has a date fairly near to that of a census year. The birth certificate of Thomas Short, for instance, provides the following information:

REGISTRATION DISTRICT Bethnal Green
1855 BIRTH in the Sub-district of *Bethnal Green* in the County of Middlesex

Where and when born	Name, if any	Sex	Name and surname of father	Name, surname and maiden name of mother	Occupation of father	Signature, description and residence of informant	When registered	Signature of registrar	Name entered after registration
31st Dec. 1855 9, Hague St.	Thomas William	Boy	Thomas Short	Sarah Short formerly Crandell	Dairyman	Thomas Short Father 9. Hague St. Bethnal Green	31st Dec. 1855	James Briggs Registrar	

The census return for the household at 9, Hague Street in 1851 (HO 107/1541 f. 288) shows that Thomas William was born in his grandparents' house, that his father and grandfather were also born in Bethnal Green; it gives the names, ages, occupations and places of birth of his grandparents and his father's brothers and sisters. This takes the 'tree' back in one step to 1797 and the next stage is to search for the baptism of Thomas William's grandfather in the East London parish registers.

The 1841 Census is not as informative as the others: it does not give the relationship of the occupants to the head of the household: it states whether or not an individual was born in the county where he was living in 1841, but not his place of birth; and ages are rounded off to the nearest five years below. More information about the census is available in PRO Guide no. 18. The PRO will do a search of a small area for a fee, and supply the required information if found. The PRO cannot supply photocopies of Census returns unless the full reference is given, the name of the place is not enough. Instruction sheets are available from the Census Room (Reference Guide no. 19).

A number of family history societies are in the process of compiling name indexes to the 1851 census. A list of areas covered is displayed in the census room.

For a fee, the General Register Office, Office of Population Censuses and Surveys will make a search in the returns for 1891 and 1901 to establish the age and place of birth of named persons, the exact address must be given. Such searches are made only for direct descendants or persons acting on their behalf, who should apply to the Director and Registrar General.

The Genealogical Society of Utah will loan microfilm copies of Census returns for indexing purposes.

See also IV/9, 10 below for Irishmen and Scotsmen; and plates.

Bibliography

Books

M W Beresford, 'The unprinted Census Returns for 1841, 1851 and 1861 for England and Wales', *Amateur Historian,* V (1963), pp. 260–269
The Census and Social Structure, an Interpretative Guide to Nineteenth Century Censuses, for England and Wales, ed. R Lawton (London, 1978)
J S W Gibson and C Chapman, ed., *Census Indexes and Indexing,* (Federation of Family History Societies, 1983)
J S W Gibson, *Census Returns on Microfilm, A Directory to Local Holdings* (Banbury, 1982)

Unpublished Finding Aids

Searching the Census, PRO Reference Guide no. 18
E McLaughlin, The Censuses 1841–1871 (1979) (from Mrs McLaughlin, Varneys, Rudds Lane, Haddenham, Bucks HP17 8JP)

Records

Home Office
HO 107   Census Papers: Population Returns, 1841 and 1851

General Register Office
RG 9   1861 Census Returns
RG 10   1871 Census Returns
RG 11   1881 Census Returns

3 Wills and other Probate Records

Wills and related documents can be very useful to the genealogist. As well as bringing characters to life, a will often provides a complete picture of the family, and bequests to local charities can be a clue to origins. Wills are, however, notoriously difficult to locate. It should be remembered that only a small proportion of the population made wills, and probably many of them went unproven; for an even smaller number were letters of administration taken out. Married women did not usually make wills before 1882 unless they were widowed. The mass of the working poor never went near a court of probate.

a After 1858

Wills proved from 12 January 1858 to the present day are no problem. They may be read (for a small fee) at the Principal Registry of the Family Division between 10.00 a.m. and 4.30 p.m., Monday to Friday. The same applies to letters of administration (granted if no will was made or could be found), but it is not worth paying the fee to read the original administration act book as it contains no more than does the index entry. Copies of wills are obtainable, either in person or by post, provided you know the date of death. Applications should be addressed to the Record Keeper, Correspondence Department; a handling charge is payable in addition to the copying charge.

If probate was issued from a district registry, you can inspect the will there if it is more convenient than going to Somerset House. The Registry has no details of the estate other than those which appear in the will or administration. For more detailed information you apply to the Capital Taxes Office.

b Before 1858

Before the Principal Probate Registry (now the Principal Registry of the Family Division) was set up, wills were usually proved in the church courts, of which there was a multiplicity. By and large the wills of ordinary people, where they exist, can be found in county record offices, but it may well be necessary to search through the records of several courts before any particular will is found. (See bibliography for printed guides to the whereabouts of wills.) For the period 1796–1858 the Death Duty Registers are the best means of locating a will (see p. 14).

c Wills in the PRO

The PRO holds the wills proved in the senior probate court for the province of Canterbury, the Prerogative Court of Canterbury (known as the PCC). These are mainly the wills of fairly substantial people living in the south of England, although by the nineteenth century those of people of smaller means may be found in the PCC. The records cover the period 1384 to 1858, and, as many of the finding aids are not arranged in a strictly alphabetical order, a search may be a long job if the date of death is not known. The Society of Genealogists will do a paid search of the indexes for the period 1750–1800, for that part of the alphabet not covered by the printed indexes.

Once found, the will may be read on a microfilm of the contemporary court copy (PROB 11) of the original will, made when probate was granted. If, however, you wish to look at the original (PROB 10) for the purpose of inspecting the seal or signature, you will have to give a week's notice. Before the mid seventeenth century, the original will was often given back to the executor, so that even if you manage to find a so-called original will, it may in fact be another court copy. Beware of attaching too much importance to the seal; many testators and witnesses just took the nearest seal to hand, which often belonged to a notary's or solicitor's clerk. Relationships described in wills may not be what they seem: 'sons' may be sons-in-law, 'cousins' may be any relative, 'nieces' and 'nephews' may be grandchildren. It should also be borne in mind that a man's will did not necessarily include all the provisions he made for his children, which often involved marriage and pre-death settlements. This was particularly true of the gentry, especially in the eighteenth century, the heyday of the 'strict settlement'. Dispositions of land were not, in any case, the concern of the church courts and may therefore be omitted from pre-1858 wills. The place to look for settlements and dispositions outside the will is among private collections, and if you are lucky there may be an Estate Act of Parliament among the Local and Personal Acts.

If there is no will to be found, it may mean that letters of administration (usually abbreviated to 'admon.') were issued, but do not be too sure of this. Often people did not bother to take them out unless they needed a legal title to the deceased's estate for the purpose of claiming a legacy due to the intestate, or the like. The original letters were kept by the administrator and can only be seen in private collections. What there is in the PRO is an entry in a register (PROB 6, PROB 7) giving the date of the grant, the name of the administrator and his relationship to the intestate, and, after 1796, the value of the personal estate. These valuations take no account of any real estate that the deceased might have had. Administrators were required to enter into a bond; this document may supply some extra information. Bonds certainly give the name of the person or persons who stood security with the administrator, and give some idea of the value of the estate. PCC bonds (PROB 46 and PROB 51) are not, however, available for inspection yet, but it is hoped that they will be released in batches as editorial and conservation work is finished. Warrants authorising the issue of letters of administration often give the date of death and sometimes a valuation of the estate (PROB 14).

There are many classes of PCC records which provide a wealth of genealogical information. Inventories of estates (see plate V) give a particularly vivid picture of the domestic scene of our ancestors, although, once again, all reference to the deceased's real estate is often omitted (PROB 2–PROB 5, PROB 31, PROB 32, PROB 37). Unfortunately, there is a relatively small number of PCC inventories, and, in particular, very few from before 1660 or after the end of the seventeenth century. Many were lost in the Great Fire and Interregnum, and the court ceased to call for them as a matter of course in the eighteenth century.

If an estate was subject to litigation in either the PCC or Chancery, there may be a great variety of documentation; depositions of witnesses (C21–C 24, PROB 24, PROB 28, PROB 31, PROB 37 and PROB 47) may be especially interesting. You should first ascertain from the various indexes, or from the sentences in the will calendars (PROB 12), whether there was litigation, then look at the classes of exhibits (PROB 31, PROB 36, PROB 37), depositions and cause papers, allegations (PROB 18) and answers (PROB 25).

The Death Duty Registers (IR 26, IR 27) are very useful as a means of discovering where a will was proved or administration granted, and thus where the records now are. They also give some further information about the estate and the legatees; the address of the executor is given. Not all wills, however, are included as some estates were of insufficient value to attract tax. There are no registers available after 1903.

For personal searchers, probate records are available in the PRO search rooms. In response to postal applications, the PRO will make a free search in the will and administration calendars, covering a period of three years from the date of death. Only three will searches should be asked for at a time. If the search is successful, an estimate is sent to the applicant of the cost of supplying photocopies.

Wills are to be found scattered throughout the public records. Among the papers of the Bona Vacanti division of the Treasury Solicitor's Office (TS 17) there are records relating to intestates' estates which escheated to the Crown, there being no next of kin, a common fate for the personal estates of unmarried bastards. There are a number of pedigrees among these papers.

For wills of Irishmen and Scots see IV/9, 10 below.

Bibliography

Books

A J Camp, *Wills and their Whereabouts* (4th edn., London, 1974)
English Probate Jurisdictions, leaflets with maps (Genealogical Society of the Church of Jesus Christ of Latter Day Saints)
J S W Gibson, *Wills and where to find them* (London, 1974)
J S W Gibson, *A Simplified Guide to Probate Jurisdictions, Where to Look for Wills* (Federation of Family History Societies, 1982)
J Cox, 'A Note on the Death Duty Registers', *Genealogists' Magazine,* Vol. XX no. 8 (Dec. 1981) pp. 261–3
J Cox, *The Records of the Prerogative Court of Canterbury* (PRO Provisional Guide, revised ed., 1984)

Published Finding Aids

Administrations in the Prerogative Court of Canterbury, 1559–1571, 1572–1580, ed. R M Glencross (Exeter, 1912, 1917), *1620–1630,* ed. J H Morrison (London, 1935)
Administrations in the Prerogative Court of Canterbury, 1581–1595, ed. C H Ridge (1954), *1596–1608, 1609–1619,* ed. M Fitch (1964–1968), *1649–1654,* ed. J Ainsworth (1944), *1655–1660,* ed. C H Ridge (1949–1953), (London, British Record Society, Index Library)
An index to administrations, 1661–1700, will be published shortly by the British Record Society
PCC Will Index, 1750–1800, vol. 1, *A–Bh* (1976), vol. II, *Bi–Ce* (1977), ed. A J Camp (London, Society of Genealogists)

P W Coldham, *English Estates of American Colonists* (Baltimore, 1980) (PCC
Wills and Admons., 1600–1699, 1700–1799 and 1800–1858)

Prerogative Court of Canterbury Sentences, 1630–1639, ed. J and G F Matthews
(London, 1907)

Prerogative Court of Canterbury Wills, vols. I and II, *1383–1558*, ed. J C C Smith
(1893–1895), vol. III, *1558–1583*, ed. S A Smith and L L Duncan (1898)
vol. IV, *1584–1604*, ed. S A Smith and E A Fry (1901), vol. V, *1605–1619*,
ed. E Stokes (1912), vol. VI, *1620–1629*, vol. VII, *1653–1656*, ed. R H E Hill
(1912, 1925), vol. VIII, *1657–1660*, ed. T M Blagg (1936), vol. IX,
1671–1675, ed, J. Ainsworth (1942), vol. X, *1676–1685*, vol. XI, 1686–1693,
ed. C H Ridge (1948, 1955–1956), vol. XII, *1694–1700*, ed. M Fitch
(1959–1960), (London, British Record Society, Index Library)

Probate Acts in the Prerogative Court of Canterbury, vol. I, *1630–1639* (1903), vol.
II, *1640–1644* (1905), vol. III, *1645–1647* (1906), vol. IV, *1648–1647* (1906),
vol. V, *1650–1651* (1909), vol. VI, *1652–1653* (1911), ed. J and G F Matthews
(London)

Wills in the Public Record Office (Baltimore, 1968) (a list of a few wills found in
various record groups (non PCC))

Unpublished Finding Aids

Card indexes of estates litigated in the PCC, 1666–1713 and PCC pleadings,
1661–c. 1800

Card index of PCC Wills 1721–1725, Society of Genealogists

Indexes to Cause Papers (PROB 28 and PROB 37)

Indexes to disputed estates in Chancery, 1575–1714, compiled by P W Coldham,
MS, by name of deceased

Indexes to PCC Exhibits, 1722–1858, photo-copy (PROB 33)

Indexes to PCC Wills, 1700–1858, MS (PROB 12)

Lists of Inventories, TS (card indexes available on request)

Records

Chancery
C21   Depositions taken by Commission (Country Depositions), Elizabeth I
to Charles I
C 22   Country Depositions, 1649–1714
C 23   Sealed Depositions, Elizabeth I to Victoria
C 24   Town Depositions, 26 Henry VIII to 1853

Inland Revenue Office
IR 26   Estate Duty Office, Death Duty Registers, 1796–1903
IR 27   Indexes to Death Duty Registers, 1796–1903

Prerogative Court of Canterbury
PROB 2   Inventories, 1464–1660
PROB 3   Inventories, 1718–1782
PROB 4   Parchment Inventories, 1661–1720 (card index available)
PROB 5   Paper Inventories, 1661–1732
PROB 6   Administration Act Books, 1559–1858

PROB 7   Act Books, Limited Administrations, 1810–1858
PROB 8   Probate Act Books, 1526–1858
PROB 9   Act Books, Limited Probates, 1781–1858
PROB 10   Original Wills, 1383–1858
PROB 11   Registered Copy Wills, 1383–1858
PROB 12   Register Books (indexes of wills and administrations), 1383–1858
PROB 14   Warrants, 1666–1858
PROB 18   Allegations, 1661–1858
PROB 24   Depositions, 1657–1809
PROB 25   Answers, 1664–1854
PROB 26   Depositions, bound by Suit, 1826–1857
PROB 28   Cause Papers, 1642–1722
PROB 31   Exhibits, 1722–1858 (indexes in PROB 33, and index of inventories
          available on request)
PROB 32   Filed exhibits with Inventories, c. 1661–c. 1700
PROB 33   Indexes to exhibits, 1683–1858 (PROB 31, PROB 37)
PROB 36   Exhibits, 1653–1721 (card index available on request)
PROB 37   Cause papers, 1783–1858
PROB 46   Administration Bonds
PROB 47   Proctors' Case Papers*
PROB 51   Administration Bonds, Sixteenth Century

Treasury Solicitor
TS 17   Bona Vacantia Division: Papers, 1808–1964

4 Records of Change of Name

Until the nineteenth century many people used aliases without going through
any legal formality. From the late nineteenth century deeds poll were often,
although not always, enrolled, and these enrolments may be seen at the PRO
(C 54, J 18). Since 1914, all enrolled deeds poll have been published in the
London Gazette, but for changes of name in the last three years, apply to
Room 81, Royal Courts of Justice. For deeds poll that were not enrolled, look
in the local and national press, and if all else fails your family solicitor may be
able to help.

Bibliography

Published Finding Aids

An Index to Change of Names, 1760–1901, ed. W P W Phillimore and E A Fry
    (London, 1905)
London Gazette (1665 to date)
J F Josling, *Change of Name*, Oyez Practice Notes I (London 1978,
    ed. 14)

---

*This class is not yet available

Unpublished Finding Aids

Indexes to Deed Poll Enrolments, MS

Records

Chancery
C 54   Close Rolls, 6 John 1903

Supreme Court of Judicature
J 18   Enrolment Books, 1903–1957

5 Apprenticeship Records

The training of working men was not usually recorded and indentures of
apprenticeship were private documents. If they survive at all they will
normally be in private hands; there is a small collection at the Society of
Genealogists. Between 1710 and 1811, however, apprenticeship indentures
were subject to tax and the records relating to this tax are in the PRO (IR 1,
indexes in IR 17). Duty was payable by the master at the rate of 6*d.* for
every £1 under £50 which he received for taking on the apprentice, and 1*s.*
for every £1 above that sum. The deadline for payment was one year after the
expiry of the indenture; it may therefore be necessary to search the records of
several years' payments in order to find a particular entry, even when the date
of the indenture is known.

The Apprenticeship Books record the names, addresses and trades of the
masters, the names of the apprentices and dates of their indentures. Until
1752 the names of apprentices' parents are given, but after that year, rarely.
There are indexes of masters' names from 1710 to 1762, and of apprentices'
names from 1710 to 1774. These were made on behalf of the Society of
Genealogists and copied from the originals in the Guildhall Library, London.
Further indexes, for later dates, are in preparation.

Where the stamp duty was paid in London, entries will be found in the 'City'
registers in this series; where it was paid elsewhere, entries will be found in the
'Country' registers.

It is important to note that masters did not have to pay stamp duty for
apprentices taken on at the common or public charge of any township or
parish, or by or out of any public charity (8 Anne, c. 5, s. 50). This means
that very many apprentices were never subject to the duty, and are therefore
not mentioned in the registers. In such cases, local or charity records, if they
survive, are likely to be the only source of information on individuals. London
Livery Companies keep full records of membership, which give places of
birth, previous residences and other details. For these, apply to the Guildhall
Library. Among the War Office records there is a list of apprentices who
enlisted in the Army but had to return to their masters until their indentures
expired, 1806 to 1835 (WO 25/2962).

a Naval Apprentices

Information about dockyard workers and other naval apprentices may be found among the Admiralty and Navy Board Correspondence (ADM 1, ADM 106). You should look under the headings 'Boys' (code 13) and 'Apprentices in Dockyards' (code 41.16) in the Admiralty Digest (ADM 12). There are Apprenticeship Registers for Greenwich Hospital for the years 1808 to 1838 (ADM 73/421, 448). Marks and results of examinations for dockyard and artificer apprentices from 1876 are to be found among the records of the Civil Service Commission (CSC 10).

b Merchant Naval Apprentices

There are indexes of apprentices registered in the Merchant Service between 1824 and 1953 (BT 150). The earlier volumes give name, date and terms of indenture and the name of the master. Entries in later volumes include the port where the apprentice signed on and the ship's name.

Bibliography

Books

W B Stephens, *Sources for English Local History* (Manchester, 1973)

Published Finding Aids

Alphabetical Guide to War Office and Other Material, PRO Lists and Indexes, vol. LIII.

Records

Admiralty
ADM 1   Admiralty and Secretariat Papers, 1660–1969
ADM 12   Admiralty and Secretariat Indexes and Compilations, Series III, 1660–1938
ADM 73/   Greenwich Hospital Registers, Boys Apprenticed, Lower School,
421, 448   1808–1838; Girls Apprenticed, 1808–1837
ADM 106 Navy Board Records, 1659–1837

Registrar General of Shipping and Seamen
BT 150   Index of Apprentices, 1824–1953

Civil Service Commission
CSC 10   Examination, Tables of Marks and Results, 1876–1959

Inland Revenue Office
IR 1   Apprenticeship Books, 1710–1811
IR 17   Indexes to Apprenticeship Books, 1710–1774

War Office
WO 25/2962   Recruits claimed as apprentices, 1806–1835

6 Tax Records

Tax records in the PRO of most use to the genealogist are the Hearth Tax returns and assessments of 1662–1674. These relate to the levy of two shillings on every hearth and are found in the class of Lay Subsidies (E 179). The class also contains a number of earlier tax returns and assessments and some of these include lists of names; where they do, the fact is noted in the class list. The list of contributors to the "Free and Voluntary Present" to Charles II in 1662 provides names and occupations or status of the more substantial members of society. About half the numbers who paid Hearth Tax subscribed to the "Present". Returns for Surrey have been published. The most complete Hearth Tax records are those for 25 March 1664. Information supplied includes names of householders, sometimes their status, and the number of hearths for which they were chargeable. The number of hearths is a clue to wealth and status. Over seven hearths usually indicates gentry and above; between four and seven hearths are wealthy craftsmen and tradesmen, merchants and yeomen; between two and three are most craftsmen, tradesmen and yeomen; the labouring poor, husbandmen and poor craftsmen usually only had one hearth. There are many gaps in the records, partly because of the loss of documentation, but partly also owing to widespread evasion of this most unpopular tax. The indexes in the PRO are arranged topographically. Hearth Tax returns for particular areas have been published by many local record societies (see card index of records in print), and some records are to be found in county record offices, among the quarter sessions records.

The parish lists of contributors to the fund for the relief of protestant refugees from Ireland in 1642 provide a number of names; but survival is patchy (SP 28/191–195, E 179). The Surrey lists are very good and a typescript list and index is available.

Land Tax assessments may be found in county record offices for the period 1780–1832. In the PRO are the Land Tax Redemption Office Quotas and Assessments (IR 23). They list all owners of property subject to Land Tax in England and Wales in 1798–1799. The arrangement is by Land Tax parish and there is no index of names. In 1798 the Land Tax became a fixed annual charge and many people purchased exemption. The records of these transactions are also useful and may include maps and plans (IR 22, IR 24). The arrangement is by parish.

The Land Revenue Commission Field Books (IR 58) give the names of all freeholders and details of the property they held from 1910 to 1913. The arrangement is topographical and the means of reference, which are the maps, are kept at present in the District Valuation Offices, and in many cases also in county record offices. You should look at these maps before visiting the PRO.

Bibliography

Books

L M Marshall, 'The Levying of the Hearth Tax 1662–1668', *English Historical Review*, vol. 51 (1936), pp. 628–646
C A F Meekings, *Introduction to The Surrey Hearth Tax, 1664*, Surrey Record Society 17 (1940)

Published Finding Aids

J Gibson, *Hearth Tax Returns and other later Stuart Tax Lists,* (Federation of
Family History Societies, 1984)
J Gibson and Dennis Mills, *Land Tax Assessments c. 1690–c. 1950,* (Federation of
Family History Societies, 1983)
C Webb and East Surrey Family History Society, *Surrey Contributors to the
relief of Protestant Refugees from Ireland, 1642*
C Webb, *Calendar of the Surrey Portion of the Free and Voluntary Present to
Charles II,* (West Surrey Family History Society, Record Series, No 2, 1982)

Unpublished Finding Aids

PRO card index of records in print
List of Exchequer K R Subsidy Rolls etc, Lay Series, vols. I–IX
(topographical arrangement, TS)

Records

Exchequer: The King's Remembrancer
E 179   Subsidy Rolls, c. Henry II to William and Mary

Inland Revenue Office
IR 22   Land Tax Redemption Office, Parish Books of Redemptions, 1799–1953
IR 23   Land Tax Redemption Office, Quotas and Assessments, 1789–1801,
1828–1914
IR 24   Land Tax Redemption Office, Registers of Redemption Certificates,
1799–1963
IR 58   Valuation Office, Field Books, 1910–1913

State Paper Office
SP 28/191–195 Commonwealth Exchequer Papers

7 Deeds and other Records of Landownership

In England and Wales, records of landownership and transfer are difficult to
locate. There was no national system of registration before the nineteenth
century. Registries of deeds were established in the three ridings of Yorkshire
and in Middlesex early in the eighteenth century; the one in Middlesex closed
in 1940, those in Yorkshire continued to operate until the 1970s. The
Middlesex register can be seen at the Greater London Record Office, those
for the north, east and west ridings of Yorkshire are in the county record
offices at Northallerton, Beverley and Wakefield. In the City of London and
in many other cities and boroughs, transfers of property were often entered
on the hustings rolls or the records of the municipal courts. These should be
sought in the relevant local record offices.

In 1862 a national Land Registry was established, but registration was
voluntary and was little used. Compulsory registration on sale was introduced
in London in 1899 and now covers all the major conurbations, but some rural
areas are still excluded and there are still many unregistered properties in the

compulsory registration areas. The Land Registry does not normally hold original deeds once property has been registered and cannot give details about the property without the permission of the current owner. Information should be sought from the relevant District Land Registry.

In the period before the nineteenth century, a high proportion of people held land by a form of tenure called copyhold. Such land was transferred by surrendering it to the lord of the manor from whom it was held; he then regranted it. Conveyances of copyhold property and the admissions of heirs on the death of tenants were entered on manorial court rolls. They are potentially a valuable source for confirming or expanding information found in parish registers which, in some cases, they predate. Court rolls, however, have a limited value for two reasons. First, there might be several manors in one parish or the property of a manor could be scattered through several parishes and consequently it is not always easy to discover of which, if any, manor a man was tenant. Secondly, the survival of court rolls has not been very good; only a small proportion of rolls survive from before the sixteenth century. Court rolls are held in the PRO and in many other repositories. A register of all surviving manorial documents is held by the Historical Manuscripts Commission. In the nineteenth century, much copyhold property was converted to freehold and copyhold was finally abolished by the Law of Property Acts, 1922 and 1924. The PRO holds lists of copyholders who converted to freehold and files relating to such cases (MAF 9, MAF 13, MAF 20, MAF 27).

The PRO has many thousands of property records, but there is no general index and searching is difficult without some idea as to when a conveyance took place. The largest series of records are the Feet of Fines (CP 25) and Common Recoveries (CP 40 and CP 43). Fines and recoveries were methods of conveying property by means of fictitious legal actions. The intended purchaser, as plaintiff, claimed the property from the vendor; the property was then transferred by a legally sanctioned agreement in the case of a fine, or by judgement of the court in the case of a recovery. Fines were used from the twelfth century until 1833, recoveries from the fifteenth century until the same date. There are manuscript lists of fines and recoveries arranged by date. Many early fines have been published, mainly by local record societies.

Until the nineteenth century it was a common practice to enrol private deeds in the central courts; certain types of deed continued to be enrolled up to 1925. The greatest number of deeds was enrolled in the Chancery (C 54); others were enrolled in the Exchequer (E 13, E 159, E 315 and E 368), the Court of Common Pleas (CP 40 before Easter 1583 and 1834–1875 and CP 43, 1583 to 1834) and the Court of King's Bench (KB 26, KB 27 before 1702 and KB 122, 1702–1875). In many cases, there are lists and indexes of such deeds. Deeds were sometimes used as evidence in law suits and their texts can be found on the plea rolls or pleading of the courts (see below, section 8).

There are many original deeds in the PRO. Most came into the crown's hands when it acquired property or were produced as evidence in law suits. There is no union list or index of them and a search would have to be made through a large number of individual class lists.

Information about properties, including the names of owners and tenants, can often be discovered from rentals and surveys in the PRO. Surveys of crown property were taken for the purpose of estate management, and private property was sometimes surveyed if it was the subject of litigation. Rentals and surveys are found among the records of the Exchequer (E 36, E 142, E 164 and E 315) and the State Paper Office (SP 10 – SP 18 and SP 46) and in Special Collections (SC 11 and SC 12). They range from the thirteenth to the nineteenth centuries, but most are from the sixteenth and seventeenth. Of special interest are the detailed Parliamentary Surveys (E 317) of the crown lands taken in the Commonwealth period. Surveys taken as a result of litigation or for other reasons will be found in the Exchequer classes Depositions by Commission (E 134) and Special Commissions (E 178) which exist for the sixteenth to the nineteenth centuries. There are published lists of all the surveys.

Many properties have, at some time, been in the hands of the crown, and, especially in the sixteenth century, many people were tenants of crown properties. If there is any evidence to suggest that a piece of property was in the crown's hands or that a person was a crown tenant, it is worth exploring the records of the royal properties; but they are voluminous and difficult to use and specialist advice should be sought.

There is one further valuable source for the period before 1600. Property held by tenure in chief, as much was, could only lawfully be sold with the crown's permission which was granted in the form of a 'licence to alienate'. Copies of the licences were enrolled on the Patent Rolls (C 66) of which there are printed calendars for the period 1216 to 1578. A search through the indexes to the calendars is an easy, and often rewarding, way of searching for early conveyances.

The palatinates of Chester (CHES), Durham (DURH) and Lancaster (PL) had their own administrations which paralleled the central government. Fines, recoveries, enrolments and deeds relating to property in those areas should be sought among their records.

Bibliography

Books and Articles

A A Dibben, *Title Deeds* (Historical Association, Helps for Students of History, no. 72, 1968)

J H Harvey, *Sources for the History of Houses* (British Records Association, Archives and the User, no. 3, 1974)

F Sheppard and V Belcher, 'The deeds registries of Yorkshire and Middlesex,' *Journal of the Society of Archivists,* vol. 6, 1978–1981, pp. 274–286

A W B Simpson, *An Introduction to the History of the Land Law* (Oxford, 1961)
A Travers, 'Manorial Documents', *Genealogists' Magazine*, vol. 21, 1983, pp. 1–10

Published Finding Aids

Catalogue of Ancient Deeds, before c. 1603 (London, 1890–1915)
Exchequer, Augmentation Office, Ancient Deeds Series B (E 326/4233-12950),
    calendar and index (List and Index Society, vols. 95, 101, 113, 124), and
    Series BB (E 328), list and index (List and Index Society, vol. 137)
Exchequer (KR), Ancient Deeds Series DD (E 211), list and index (List and Index
    Society, vol. 200)
Exchequer (LR), Ancient Deeds Series E (LR 14), list (List and Index Society,
    vol. 181)
Exchequer (TR), Ancient Deeds Series A (E 40/13673–15910), list (List and
    Index Society, vols. 151, 152) and *Series AS and WS (E 42, E 43)*, list (List and
    Index Society, vol. 158)
Calendar of Patent Rolls, Henry III to Henry VII and Edward VI to 1578 (London
    1891–1982)
Letters and Papers, Foreign and Domestic, Henry VIII (London, 1864–1910),
    includes Patent Rolls
Chancery Patent Rolls, contemporary calendars, 1–15 James I (List and Index
    Society, vols. 97, 98, 109, 121, 122, 133, 134, 157, 164, 187, 193)
List of Rentals and Surveys and other analogous Documents, (PRO Lists and
    Indexes, XXV)
List of Special Commissions and Returns in the Exchequer, (PRO Lists and Indexes,
    XXXVII)
Calendar of Depositions taken by Commission, *Deputy Keeper's Report XXXVIII*,
    Appendix 2: 1 Eliz. I to 22 James I; *XXXIX*, Appendix 2: 1–24 Charles I; *XL*,
    Appendix 1: 24 Charles I to 4 James II; *XLI*, Appendix 1: 1 William and Mary
    to 13 George I; *XLII*, Appendix 1: George II

Unpublished Finding Aids

Catalogue of Lists and Indexes, sections relating to Exchequer, King's Bench
    and Common Pleas, (TS (for indexes to Plea and Recovery Rolls)
Indexes to the Close Rolls, MS
Lists and Indexes of Ancient Deeds, TS
Lists and Indexes of Enrolled Deeds, TS
Lists of Feet of Fines, MS

Records

Chancery
C 54   Close Rolls 1204–1903

Court of Common Pleas
CP 25   Feet of Fines, Henry II to 1839
CP 40   Plea Rolls, 1272–1875   (indexes in IND 1–6605)
CP 43   Recovery Rolls, 1582–1837   (indexes in IND 17183–17216)

Palatinate of Chester
CHES 2   Enrolments, 1307–1830

CHES 29   Plea Rolls, Chester, 1255–1831
CHES 30   Plea Rolls, Flint, 1283–1831
CHES 31   Fines and Recoveries, 1280–1831
CHES 32   Enrolments of Fines and Recoveries, 1585 to Anne

Duchy of Lancaster
DL 25   Deeds (12th to 17th century), Series L
DL 26   Deeds, Series LL
DL 27   Deeds, Series LS
DL 32   Parliamentary Surveys, Commonwealth
DL 42   Miscellaneous Books, John to 1835
DL 43   Rentals and Surveys, Henry III to George III
DL 44   Special Commissions and Returns, 1558–1853

Palatinate of Durham
DURH 12   Feet of Fines, 1535–1834
DURH 13   Judgement Rolls, 1344–1845
DURH 21   Deeds, Series G, 17th century

Exchequer: Exchequer of Pleas
E 13   Plea Rolls, 1235–1875

Exchequer: Treasury of Receipt
E 40   Ancient Deeds, (12th century to 1603), Series A
E 41   Ancient Deeds, Series AA
E 42   Ancient Deeds, Series AS
E 43   Ancient Deeds, Series WS
E 44   Modern Deeds, 17th century

Exchequer: King's Remembrancer
E 134   Depositions by Commission, Elizabeth I to Victoria
E 142   Ancient Extents, John to Henry VI
E 159   Memoranda Rolls, 1217–1959
E 164   Miscellaneous Books, Series I, Henry III to 1797
E 178   Special Commissions of Inquiry, Elizabeth I to Victoria

Exchequer: Augmentation Office
E 315   Miscellaneous Books, 12th to 18th century
E 326   Ancient Deeds, (12th century to 1603), Series B
E 327   Ancient Deeds, Series BX
E 328   Ancient Deeds, Series BB
E 329   Ancient Deeds, Series BS
E 330   Modern Deeds, Series B, after 1603

Exchequer: Lord Treasurer's Remembrancer
E 368   Memoranda Rolls, 1217–1835

Exchequer: Office of the Auditors of Land Revenue
LR 2   Miscellaneous Books, Henry V to 1841
LR 14   Ancient Deeds, Series E, Henry III to Elizabeth I
LR 15   Ancient Deeds, Series EE, 15th to 17th century
LR 16   Modern Deeds, Series E, 17th to 18th century

Court of King's Bench
KB 26   Curia Regis Rolls, 1193–1272
KB 27   Coram Rege Rolls, 1273–1702
KB 122   Judgement Rolls, 1702–1875

Ministry of Agriculture, Fisheries and Food
MAF 9   Deeds and Awards of Enfranchisement, 1841–1925
MAF 13   Extinguishment of Manorial Incidents, Series I, 1926–1944
MAF 20   Manor Files, 1840–1900
MAF 27   Extinguishment of Manorial Incidents, Series II, 1936–1957

Palatinate of Lancaster
PL 2   Close Rolls, 1409–1470
PL 14   Chancery Miscellanea, Richard II to Victoria
PL 15   Plea Rolls, 1400–1848
PL 17   Fines, 1362–1834
PL 29   Deeds, Series H, 16th to 19th century

Principality of Wales
WALE 29   Ancient Deeds, Series F, Edward I to Elizabeth I
WALE 30   Ancient Deeds, Series FF, Elizabeth I
WALE 31   Modern Deeds, after 1603

8 Legal Proceedings

The PRO holds records of all the central law courts, including the records of
assize circuits (ASSI). The records of some of the county courts (AK) are also
there, beginning in the 1840s. Records of quarter sessions are held locally;
many have been calendared and are in print. If you are embarking on a hunt
for anything you can find about your ancestors, without definite information
about any specific suit, it is probably best to start with quarter sessions
records.

By and large the records of the central courts of common law are best
avoided; they are difficult to read and understand, and not particularly fruitful.
Means of reference, where they exist, may be complicated. If searching for a
specific case, you must know the name of the plaintiff, the date, and the court
where the action took place. For the nineteenth century you will invariably
find reports printed in newspapers much more informative than the extant
documentation. For Sussex, Surrey, Kent, Essex and Hertfordshire there are
printed calendars of assize records, for the reigns of Elizabeth I and James I.
They are fully indexed and well worth looking at.

The records of the courts of equity, which begin in the late fourteenth
century and continue to the nineteenth, are easier to use and more
informative than those of the common law courts. There were nine courts:
Chancery (C), which handled the most business; Exchequer (E); Star
Chamber (STAC) and the Court of Requests (REQ), both of which existed
only from the late fifteenth to the mid seventeenth century; the Court of the
Duchy of Lancaster (DL); the Palatinate Courts of Lancaster (PL), Chester
(CHES) and Durham (DURH); and the Court of Augmentations (E), for

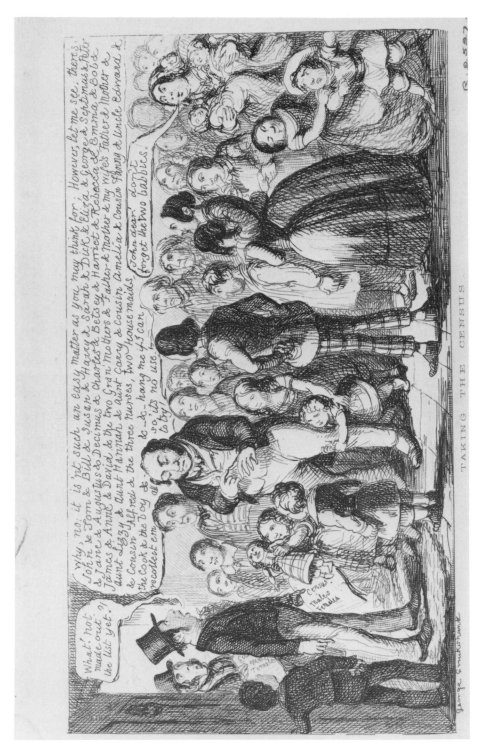

I 'Taking the Census'
Published by the Courtesy of the Trustees of the British Museum

former monastic land only. From 1873 the Chancery Division of the Supreme Court of Judicature took over all equity jurisdiction. The equity courts had written proceedings in English. They competed for business with one another, dealing with disputes over land, wills, marriage settlements, etc. There are various means of reference available in the PRO. They are mostly manuscript indexes by the name of the plaintiffs (surnames only). Because of the huge volume of business handled in Chancery, and the arrangement of the records, the search for individuals may be a protracted procedure. It is a good idea to use the microfilm of the Bernau index at the Society of Genealogists for the eighteenth century; this contains references to every Chancery litigant between 1714 and 1758, and also includes all Exchequer deponents from 1559 to 1695. There are various lists, indexes and calendars of Chancery Proceedings from the reign of Richard II to the seventeenth century. From the reign of James I until 1842 Chancery Proceedings are arranged in six concurrent series. If there is no printed or microfilm index for the period you are searching, because of this division into the Six Clerks Series you should go to the indexes to the Decree and Order Books (1544–1875). Having followed the account of the case through the Decree and Order Books you can then, if necessary, look for other proceedings: bills, answers, etc.

Disputes concerning ships or cargoes were heard in the Admiralty Court (HCA). The records of this court are not easy to use but can be very informative if a relevant case is located.

a Unclaimed Money (Dormant Funds)
Many families have stories of money "in Chancery". This may refer to money deposited by solicitors (from 1876) when they were unable to trace legatees or next of kin. For cash and securities in accounts which have not been dealt with for upward of fifteen years (England only) searches can be made free of charge in the 1922–1952 list in the Eastern Corridor, Ground Floor, Royal Courts of Justice. Enquiries should be sent to the Chief Accountant, Supreme Court Pay Office, Royal Courts of Justice; evidence of beneficial interest is required. Lists of funds published as supplements to the London Gazette (1893–1974), can be consulted in the PRO.

b Pedigrees
Pedigrees were frequently produced as evidence in law suits but, except in a few classes, it is very difficult to find them. For the eighteenth and nineteenth centuries there are manuscript indexes of pedigrees in some classes of Chancery Masters Exhibits (C 103–C 114) on the open shelves. Most of these pedigrees relate to disputed wills and administrations. A TS index to pedigrees among various Supreme Court papers is available.

For Criminal proceedings see IV/21 below.

Bibliography

Books

F G Emmison and Irvine Gray, *Survey of Quarter Sessions Records,* Historical Association Pamphlet 33 (1948)

R E F Garrett, *Chancery and other Legal Proceedings* (Shalfleet Manor, 1968)
An Introduction to Chancery Proceedings, PRO Leaflet No. 32
J S W Gibson, *Quarter Sessions Records for Family Historians,* a select list
(Federation of Family History Societies, 1982)

Published Finding Aids

Calendar of Assize Records, Hertfordshire Indictments, Elizabeth I and *James I,*
ed. J S Cockburn (London, 1975)
Calendar of Assize Records, Sussex Indictments, Elizabeth I and *James I,* ed. J S
Cockburn (London, 1975)
Calendar of Assize Records, Essex Indictments, Elizabeth I and *James I,* ed. J S
Cockburn (London, 1978 and 1982)
Calendar of Assize Records, Kent Indictments, Elizabeth I and *James I,* ed J S
Cockburn (London, 1979 and 1981)
Calendar of Assize Records, Surrey Indictments, Elizabeth I and James I, ed. J S
Cockburn, (London, 1980 and 1982)
P W Coldham, *Bonded Passengers to America* (Baltimore, 1983) List of deportees
to North America from Assize and other records
Calendar of Proceedings in Chancery in the Reign of Queen Elizabeth I ed. J Caley and
J Bayley (London, Record Commission, 1827–1832)
*Calendar of Chancery Proceedings, Bills and Answers filed in the reign of Charles
I,* vols. 1–3, ed. W P W Phillimore, vol. 4, ed. E A Fry (British Record
Society, Index Library, 1903–1904)
Index Nominum of Early Chancery Proceedings, 1386–1467, ed. C A Walmisley
(Harleian Society, vols. LXXVIII–LXXIX, 1927–1928)
Index of Chancery Proceedings, PRO Lists and Indexes, vol. VII, *1558–1579*
(1896), vol. XXIV, *1579–1621* (1908), vol. XXX, *1621–1660* (1909)
Index of Chancery Proceedings, James I, A–K only, PRO Lists and Indexes, vol.
XLVII (1922)
Index of Chancery Proceedings, 1603–1625, A–L only, ed. R Topham, *The
Genealogist,* n.s. vols. IV, VI–IX (1887, 1889–1892)
Index of Chancery Proceedings, Bridges' Division, 1613–1714, PRO Lists and
Indexes, vol. XXXIX (1913), vol. XLII (1914), vol. XLIV (1915), vol. XLV
(1917)
Index of Chancery Proceedings, Reynardson's Division, 1649–1714, ed. E A Fry
(British Record Society, Index Library, 1903–1904)
Lists of Early Chancery Proceedings, PRO Lists and Indexes, vol. XII, *9 Ric.
II–Edw. IV* (1901), vol XVI, *1467–1485* (1903), vol. XX, *1485–1500* (1906),
vol. XXIX, *1500–1515* (1908), vol. XXXVIII, *1515–1529* (1912), vol. XLVIII,
1529–1538 (1922), vol. L, *1533–1538* (1927), vol. LI, *1538–1544* (1929), vol.
LIV, *1544–1553* (1933), vol. LV, *1533–1558* (1936)
*List and Index to the Proceedings in the Star Chamber for the Reign of James I
(1603–1625) in the PRO,* ed. T G Barnes (Chicago, 1975)
Indexes to Proceedings in the Court of Requests, Henry VII to James I, PRO Lists
and Indexes, Supplementary, vol. VII (New York, 1964–1974)

Unpublished Finding Aids

Index of Chancery Proceedings, ed. C Bernau, for PRO classes C 11, C 12, C 21,

C 24, 8% of C 22 and parts of Exchequer (microfilm at the Society of Genealogists)

Index of Chancery Proceedings, James I, L–Z only, MS

Indexes to disputed estates in Chancery, Collins Division, Hamilton Division, Mitford Division, Whitington Division, 1649–1714, ed. P W Coldham, arranged by name of deceased

Indexes of Chancery Proceedings, 1714–1758, 1758–1800, 1800–1842, MS and TS

Index of Chancery Affidavits from 1615 (C 31, C 41), PRO IND 14545 *et seq.*

Index of Supreme Court Pedigrees (J 46, J 63, J 64), TS

Index of Town Depositions, Henry VIII to Mary (C 24), Deponents, IND 16759, Depositions, IND 9115–9121

Index of Country Depositions, 1649–1714 (C 11, C 12, C 21, C 22), topographical index 1714–1744, TS and MS at Society of Genealogists

Index of Decrees and Orders, 1544–1841 (C 33), IND 1388 *et seq.*

Index of Reports and Certificates, 1606–1759 (C 38), IND 1878–2028; 1760–1800, IND 10700; 1800–1841, IND 14919–14959

Index of Exchequer Deponents, 1559–1695, TS

Various indexes to Star Chamber records, 1485–James I, MS

List and index of Supreme Court Central Office documents exhibited, 19th–20th century (J 90), TS

Records

ASSI	Clerks of Assize
AK	County Courts
C	Chancery
C 103–C 114	Masters' Exhibits, 13th to 19th century
CHES	Palatinate of Chester
DURH	Palatinate of Durham
DL	Duchy of Lancaster
E	Exchequer
HCA	High Court of Admiralty
J	Supreme Court of Judicature
PL	Palatinate of Lancaster
REQ	Court of Requests
STAC	Court of Star Chamber

9 Tontines and Annuity Records

Tontines were government money raising schemes, of which there were eleven between 1693 and 1789. In return for an original investment participants were guaranteed a yearly income for the life of a living nominee chosen by the investor. People usually nominated their youngest relative. As the nominees died off, the central fund was distributed between fewer and fewer people and the annuity therefore became more valuable as the years passed. There were in all about 15,000 participants. The records (NDO 1–NDO 3) may give details concerning the marriages, deaths, and wills of contributors and nominees. Contributors were usually quite substantial people and many of them came from the south of England. Many were spinsters. The registers have integral indexes.

The records of the Irish Tontine are particularly useful because of the general dearth of Irish material (NDO 3).

Bibliography

F Leeson, *A Guide to the Records of the British State Tontines and Life Annuities of the 17th and 18th Centuries* (Shalfleet Manor, 1968)

Records

National Debt Office
NDO 1   Life Annuities (1745–1757) and Tontine (1789), 1745–1843
NDO 2   Life Annuities (1766–1779) and Tontine (1789), 1776–1888
NDO 3   Irish Tontines (1773–1777), 1773–1871

10 Tithe Records

Tithes (the tax of a tenth of all produce, payable to the local clergyman) were a source of dispute over the years. In 1836 the Tithe Commutation Act was passed and a fixed money payment was substituted. The records emanating from this procedure, in the form of maps and apportionments, copies of which are held in county record offices as well as at the PRO (IR 29, IR 30), supply names of landowners and occupiers for a large number of parishes and chapelries, with details of the holdings and a description of the state of cultivation. There were many areas where tithes had already been commuted for land or money in the course of private enclosures. For these areas there are, of course, no records in the Inland Revenue classes. Also, there were a good many districts in which, although the tithes were commuted under the provisions of the 1836 Act, no apportionment was made. This was either because the amount involved was negligible or because the landowners were themselves the tithe owners, and the agreement or award of a gross tithe rentcharge was followed by the redemption or merger of the tithe rentcharges. By this means the expense of a formal apportionment and of the preparation of a map was avoided. In such cases the result of the proceedings will be recorded in a formal agreement or instrument of merger (TITH 3), and there should be a Tithe file (IR 18) which is rarely informative.

Bibliography

Published Finding Aids

Lists of Inland Revenue Tithe Maps and Apportionments, vol. I, *Bedford to Northumberland;* vol. II *Nottingham to Yorkshire, Wales* (List and Index Society vols. 68 and 83)

Records

Inland Revenue Office
IR 18   Tithe Files 1836–c. 1870

IR 29   Tithe Redemption Office: Tithe Apportionments, 19th Century
IR 30   Tithe Redemption Office: Tithe Maps, 19th Century

Tithe Redemption Commission
TITH 1   Boundary Awards, 1839–1842, 1860
TITH 2   Sealed Originals, 1836–1866
TITH 3   Declarations of Merger, 1837–1936

11 Oath Rolls

In 1696 all office holders were required to take an oath of loyalty to the crown. The Association Oath Rolls (C 213) have the names of all MPs, freemen of City Companies, military and civil officers of the crown, clergy and gentry. The arrangement is topographical and a list of the surviving rolls has been published by C R Webb. The rolls were partially indexed by Bernau.

Bibliography

Published Finding Aids

C R Webb, 'The Association Oath Rolls of 1695', *Genealogists' Magazine*, vol. XXI no. 4 (Dec 1983) pp. 120–123

Unpublished Finding Aids

Bernau Index, Society of Genealogists

Records

C 213   Association Oath Rolls, 8 William III

12 Company Records

Information about the business activities and contacts of directors and shareholders of registered companies can be found in the wealth of records which have been created since the mid-nineteenth century. For records of live companies and of those which have ceased to function within the last 20 years, you should apply to the Companies Registration Office, in London or Cardiff. For a small fee the Office will produce for you a microfiche copy which you may keep and this will contain all the general documents relating to any one company. Other company records are held in the PRO as listed in the bibliography of records below.

The registry of business names (BT 253) may be useful; from 1916 people running businesses under names other than their own were required to register with the Board of Trade.

The records of Scottish Companies are held in Edinburgh by the Registrar of Companies; files of companies dissolved to 1969 are in the Scottish Record Office.

Bibliography

C T and M J Watts, "Company Records as a Source for the Family Historian", *Genealogists' Magazine,* vol. 21 no. 2 (June 1983) pp. 44–54

Records

Board of Trade
BT 31   Companies Registration Office Files of Dissolved Companies, 1856–1959 (Only a 1% sample of files of private companies have been retained. This class is open after five years)
BT 34   Companies Registration Office Dissolved Companies, Liquidators' Accounts, 1890–1932. (This class is open after five years)
BT 41   Companies Registration Office Files of Joint Stock Companies Registered under the 1844 and 1856 Acts, 1844–c. 1860 (Alphabetically arranged)
BT 253   Register of Business Names, sample years 1916–1961

Supreme Court
J 13   Companies (Winding-up) Proceedings, 1891–1951 (Samples only from 1949. Card index available)

IV Special groups of people

1 Soldiers

If a census return, parish register or family tradition tells you that your ancestor was a soldier, it may well be worth your while looking for his service record in the PRO. Some of these records may give information about families, domiciles and even physical descriptions. You may be started on the trail by finding out that your ancestor was a Chelsea or Kilmainham pensioner, which means he was in receipt of an army pension.

Service records of the British Army are in the PRO. There are few from before 1660, the main collection at present covering the years 1660-1913. For the period since 1913 for other ranks you should make a written application to the Ministry of Defence, but a large proportion of the records of soldiers serving between 1914 and 1920 were destroyed by bombing in the Second World War. The records of officers' services until 1954 are at the PRO, except for the Royal Artillery who have their own record office. For information about pensions of men injured in the First World War, and for relatives of those killed in action, see the records of the Paymaster General (PMG) or write to the Department of Health and Social Security in Nelson; casualty lists for the war have been published, and copies are available in the British Library or by appointment at the Imperial War Museum. There are a number of other avenues that can be explored as explained in Norman Holding's book. Information about burials in both World Wars is available from the Commonwealth War Graves Commission.

For the Second World War, the most useful sources in the PRO are the War Diaries (WO 165-WO 179) arranged by unit. You will need to sign an undertaking of confidentiality before looking at the War Diaries.

There was no regular standing army in Britain before the Civil War (1642-1649). Regiments were raised to meet special requirements and were usually known by the names of colonels who commanded them. Such references as there are to individual soldiers should be sought among the State Papers Domestic (SP), State Papers Foreign (SP) and the Exchequer and Audit Office Accounts (AO 1-AO 3). It would be unusual to find any reference in these sources to birthplace, wife or family of an individual. Other places to look might be Exchequer Issues (E 403) and Exchequer Accounts (E 101) for the payment of military wages, the State Papers (SP) for widows' pensions, the Licences to pass beyond the Seas (E 157), for oaths of allegiance taken by soldiers going to the Low Countries in 1613 to 1624, and the

Commonwealth Exchequer Papers for the army during the Interregnum
(SP 28). All Officers serving in the Civil War and Commonwealth period are
listed in Edward Peacock's book. Warrants for commissions of the
seventeenth and eighteenth centuries can be found in the State Paper Entry
Books.

a Organisation

Some basic grasp of the organisation of the army is necessary for the proper
use of military records. The army was divided into commissioned officers,
recruited from the top level of society, as they were the people who could
afford to buy commissions; and other ranks, the lowest of whom were often
drawn from the poorest classes, including criminals and paupers. Between
1780 and 1914 there was voluntary enlistment, normally for life. Whenever a
new regiment was needed a colonel was given a 'beating order' to enlist, and
recruitment headquarters were established, usually in local inns. Few soldiers
stayed the course for the whole of their life: some bought themselves out;
some were wounded, incapacitated and discharged; many were discharged at
the end of the various wars. Boys had to be eighteen before they could be
legally enlisted, but this rule was not always observed. Garrisons were
established for the quartering of troops throughout the country, and in times
of stress when the garrison troops were needed elsewhere, special battalions of
veterans would be raised to take their place. The basic unit of the army was
the regiment, under the command of a colonel, usually consisting of several
companies (or, in the cavalry, troops) of about a hundred men each. These
regiments were of various types: cavalry (on horseback), infantry (foot
soldiers), artillery (to fire the cannons) and engineers (to construct bridges,
roads and mines).

There was an army in India for many years, maintained by the East India
Company, which only become part of the British Army proper in 1859. For
records relating to soldiers in India before this date, you should apply to the
India Office Library.

b Officers

There were four sorts of officer:

general officers, who co-ordinated the efforts of the whole army: field
marshal, general, lieutenant general, major general.

regimental officers: colonel (in command of a regiment), lieutenant colonel,
major.

company officers: captain (in command of a company), and his subalterns:
lieutenant and cornet (cavalry) or ensign (infantry). Cornets and ensigns
became second lieutenants in 1871.

others: paymaster, adjutant (an administrative assistant), quartermaster (in
charge of accommodation and stores), surgeon, chaplain.

Officers should be easy to find. First look in the *Army Lists,* which begin in
1754 and are available in good libraries. There is also a manuscript regimental

list for 1702 to 1823 (WO 64). For family details you could look among the applications for commissions in Commander in Chief's Memoranda (WO 31) from 1793, and in the widow's pension applications (WO 42). Additional biographical information may be found in H G Hart's papers for the period 1838–1875 (WO 211).

Before 1829 there is no certainty of finding what you are looking for. After that date it is more likely as systematic records began to be kept. These are arranged by regiment, but some regiments' records have not been transferred to the PRO and are presumed lost. Having found your officer in the *Army List,* your next step is to consult the War Office Registers (WO 25) which contain, among other things, a series of returns of officers' services, the most useful being those for 1808–1810 (no personal details), 1829 to 1919 (officers on active service) and 1829 (retired officers). These registers are supplemented by the Records of Officers' Services, c. 1771–1954 (WO 76). There are some baptismal, marriage and death certificates for 1755 to 1908 (WO 42), and also the date of an officer's death can usually be found in the Paymaster General's Records of Full and Half Pay (PMG 3, PMG 4). As a last resort, the *Gentleman's Magazine* may be helpful. The Royal Military Academy, Sandhurst, will supply details of cadets.

c Other Ranks

The enlisted men were privates (troopers in the cavalry), trumpeters and drummers, supervised by corporals and sergeants, non-commissioned officers promoted from the ranks.

To find records relating to an ordinary soldier who was discharged to pension before 1883, unless you are prepared for a very long search indeed, you must know the name of the regiment or a campaign he fought in. Regimental names usually appear on census returns (see III/2 above), probate records (III/3 above) and Chaplains' returns (IV/16 below). After 1883 this is not necessary as the discharge papers are arranged alphabetically through the entire army. The Regular Soldiers Documents (WO 97) (see plate II) are the main series of service records and contain the details of a soldier's army service until he was discharged to pension. They cover the period 1756 to 1913, and, after 1883, contain some family details as well as personal information. You may also find something in the Medal Rolls (WO 100) if you know your ancestor fought in a particular campaign.

The records of soldiers who died in the service have not survived, so, for such men you will have to look in the Muster Books and Pay Lists (WO 10, WO 13, WO 16), which may be a lengthy task as not only are they arranged regimentally, but also each volume covers only a twelve month period. In many of these volumes, you will find a form showing 'Men becoming non-effective' at the end of each quarter. Where this exists, it should show the birthplace of the man discharged or dead, his trade and his date of enlistment. By tracing him back through the Muster Books it may be possible to find his age shown on the day of enlistment as a recruit. The Musters also contain Marriage Rolls after about 1868, which sometimes include information about children as well as wives (and see IV/16 below). The entry of a recruit in the Musters generally gives his age and the place he joined but does not give his birthplace. When the unit in which a man served is not known, but a place and date are given, you can find out which regiments were stationed there from the Monthly Returns (WO 17, WO 73). The Musters of regimental depots are usually bound in with the other musters of regiments based at home until about 1872.

i South African (Boer) War, 1899–1902
The service documents of British regular soldiers who served in South Africa were, for the most part, destroyed by enemy bombing in the Second World War. Those which survived are in the PRO. The Medal Rolls (WO 100) sometimes contain a few personal details, such as the date of discharge or death, and the home address. For the British Auxiliary Forces, you will find some records of the City Imperial Volunteers at the Guildhall Library, and the soldiers' documents of the Imperial Yeomanry are at the PRO (WO 128). You will also find enrolment forms and nominal rolls of local armed forces (WO 126, WO 127), and enlistment papers and rolls of those who took part in the campaign (WO 108).

ii American War of Independence, 1776–1783
The Muster Books and Pay Lists of many regiments that took part in this war may be found, but the discharge certificates of men discharged in North America, which give the age and place of birth, can very seldom be traced. It is unlikely that you will find anything but a man's name, rank and date of discharge in the musters. There are some pay lists and account books for Hessian troops, but they provide few personal details; some Audit Office accounts (AO 3) may be useful. The Loyalist Regiment Rolls for provincial troops are in the Public Archives of Canada.

iii India
The service records of European officers and soldiers of the Honourable East India Company's service, and of the Indian (Imperial) Army are mainly preserved at the India Office Library, but the service records of the regular army in India will be found with the other army records in the PRO. You will often find the name of the wife as next of kin in the casualty returns when a soldier has died (WO 25). There are musters of regiments in India from 1883 to 1889 (WO 16), but there are none for the Artillery or the Engineers. When a soldier was discharged on his return home, you should find a record of this in the depot musters of his regiment (WO 67), in the Musters of the Victoria Hospital, Netley (for the years 1863–1878) (WO 12) or in the Musters of the Discharge Depot, Gosport (1875–1889) (WO 16).

iv Soldiers' Wills
If a soldier died abroad before 1858 and left assets over a certain amount (this was regulated by statute) grants of probate or administration were issued in the Prerogative Court of Canterbury (*see* III/3 above). Military wills of small estates did not have to be proved in court, so there is no record of these

unless they have survived among pension applications and casualty returns in the War Office records (e.g. WO 25 and WO 42).

v Regimental Records
Most regiments have their own museums, some of which have archival collections; a search may be productive. The National Army Museum and the Army Museums Ogilby Trust also have collections.

vi Deserters
There are War Office registers of deserters (1799–1852) (WO 25) which contain personal details and the punishment awarded to deserters who were caught, and certificates among the papers of the Tax Receivers for the award of the bounty for catching deserters (from the 1720s) (E 182). Deserters are listed in the War Office records in the various returns of men becoming non-effective.

vii Chaplains
Because of the dearth of War Office records of chaplains, look first at *Crockford's Clerical Directory,* then the diocesan register of ordinands in the appropriate diocesan record office, and the Oxford and Cambridge *Alumni.* You may find something in the *Gentleman's Magazine.* In the PRO there are entries of payments to chaplains, 1805–1843 (WO 25) and letters from chaplains, 1808–1836, in the Chaplain General's Letter Books (WO 40).

viii Medals
Citations of awards (both World Wars) appear in the *London Gazette.* Information is also available from the Ministry of Defence.

ix Poles
Records of Polish servicemen fighting under British command during the Second World War are held by the Ministry of Defence.

d Other Military Formations

i The Militia
From medieval times, able-bodied men aged between 16 and 60 were liable to perform military service within their counties, and occasionally outside them, in times of need. From the 1540s, the records of musters were returned to the Secretaries of State, and many of these, with some earlier ones from 1522 onwards, are scattered among various classes in the PRO (E 36, E 101, E 315, SP 1, SP 2, SP 10, SP 12, SP 14, SP 16, SP 17). Some muster books, however, were retained by the deputy lieutenants of the counties, and these are now in private collections or county record offices.

A few militia soldiers qualified for pensions during the French Revolutionary and Napoleonic Wars, and their discharge certificates among the ordinary soldiers' documents (WO 97) give their place of birth and age on enlistment. There are also lists of militia men, and wives and children who were eligible for pensions among the subsidiary documents to the Receiver's Accounts

(E 182), but there are no indexes, so it is a question of wading through sacks of documents. You would do better to look in the War Office and Home Office records for the militia in the late eighteenth century and the nineteenth century (HO 51, WO 13, WO 68). Orders for maintenance of children of militia men may be found among locally held poor law records.

ii The Territorial Army

The Territorial Force was established in 1908 by amalgamating the Militia, Yeomanry (mounted volunteers) and Volunteer Force (infantry), to provide defences for Britain when the regular army had gone abroad. It became the Territorial Army in 1921. Most of the records are held locally; the muster rolls of some London and Middlesex Volunteer and Territorial regiments (1860–1912) are in the PRO (WO 70).

iii Military Police

The Military Police became a separate organisation from the middle of the nineteenth century, and enquiries should be sent direct to them.

iv Women's Land Army

For the service records of women recruited as agricultural labour during the Second World War, write to the Women's Land Army Benevolent Association.

See also IV/16 below for deaths abroad, and IV/24 below for prisoners of war.

Bibliography

Books

A P Bruce, *An annotated Bibliography of the British Army 1660–1714* (London, 1975)

Crockford's Clerical Directory (Oxford, from 1858)

C Firth and G Davis, *The Regimental History of Cromwell's Army* (Oxford, 1940)

J Foster, *Alumni Oxonienses, 1500–1886* (Oxford, 1891)

The Gentleman's Magazine (London, 1731–1903)

G Hamilton Edwards, *In Search of Army Ancestry* (London, 1977)

M S Giuseppi, *Guide to the Manuscripts preserved in the Public Record Office* (London, 1923–1924)

N Holding, *World War I Ancestry* (Federation of Family History Societies, 1982)

M E S Laws, *Battery Records of the Royal Artillery*, vol. I, *1716–1859*, vol. II, *1859–1877* (Woolwich, 1952, 1970)

E E Rich, 'The Population of Elizabethan England', *Economic History Review*, 2nd series, vol. II (1949–1950), pp. 247–265

A Swinson (ed), *A Register of the Regiments and Corps of the British Army, the Ancestry of the Regiments and Corps of the Regular Establishment of the Army* (London, 1975)

J and J A Venn, *Alumni Cantabrigienses, from the Earliest Times to 1900* (Cambridge, 1922–1927)

A S White, *A Bibliography of the Regiments and Corps of the British Army* (London, 1965)

T Wise, *A Guide to Military Museums* (Hemel Hempstead, 1971)

Published Finding Aids

Alphabetical Guide to War Office and other Military Records preserved in the Public Record Office, PRO Lists and Indexes, vol. LIII (1931)

The Army List (London, annually from 1754)

Calendar of State Papers, Domestic Series (London, 1856–1972)

T W J Connolly, *List of Officers, Royal Engineers, 1660–1898* (London, 1898)

C Dalton, *English Army List and Commission Registers, 1661–1714* (London, 1892–1904)

C Dalton, *Waterloo Roll* (London, 2nd edn., 1904)

E Dwelly, *Waterloo Muster Rolls: Cavalry* (Fleet, Hants, 1934)

H G Hart, *Army Lists* (from 1840)

J Kane, *List of Officers, Royal Artillery, 1716–1899* (London, 4th edn., 1900)

K O N Kingsley-Foster, *Military General Service Medal, 1793–1814* (London, 1947)

Letters and Papers of Henry VIII (London, 1920–1929) e.g. for Militia musters

Lists of War Office Records, PRO Lists and Indexes, vol. XXVIII (1908), PRO Supplementary Lists and Indexes, vol. VIII (1968)

London Gazette (1665 to date)

Officers died in the Great War (London, 1921), the Imperial War Museum, London

E Peacock, *The Army List of Roundheads and Cavaliers* (London, 2nd edn., 1874)

Soldiers died in the Great War, 80 parts (London, 1921–1922), the Imperial War Museum, London

Unpublished Finding Aids

Index to deserters' certificates for Bedfordshire, Buckinghamshire, Berkshire, Cambridgeshire, Cheshire and Middlesex, card index

Index of Names of Officers who appear in the Army Lists 1702–1752 (WO 64 and WO 65) card index

Index to Records of Officers' Services (WO 25) card index

Index to Births, Marriages and Deaths of Soldiers 1755–1908 (WO 42) TS

Records

Exchequer and Audit Department
AO 1   Declared Accounts, 1536–1828
AO 2   Declared and Passed Accounts, 1803–1848
AO 3   Accounts, Various, 1539–1886

Exchequer: Treasury of Receipt
E 36   Books, 13th to 18th century (Militia musters, E 36/16–55a)

Exchequer: King's Remembrancer
E 101   Various Accounts, Henry II to George III (Militia musters, E 101/58 *et seq.,* 549)

E 157   Licences to pass beyond the Seas, Elizabeth I to 1677
E 182   Receivers' Accounts of Land and Assessed Taxes: Subsidiary Documents, 1689–1830

Exchequer: Augmentation Office
E 315   Miscellaneous Books, 12th to 18th century (Militia musters, E 315/464, 466)

Exchequer of Receipt
E 403   Enrolments and Registers of Issues, Henry III to 1834

Home Office
HO 51   Military Entry Books, 1782–1840

Paymaster General's Office
PMG 3   Army Establishment, Retired Full Pay and General Officers' Pay and Allowances, 1813–1920
PMG 4   Army Establishment Half Pay, 1737–1921
PMG 5   Commissariat Half Pay, Pensions, etc., 1854–1855
PMG 6   Army Establishment, Foreign Half Pay, Pensions, etc., 1822–1885
PMG 7   Army Establishment, Hanover, Foreign Half Pay, Pensions, etc., 1843–1862
PMG 8   Army Establishment, Hanover, Chelsea Out-Pensions, 1844–1877
PMG 9   Army Establishment, Pensions for Wounds, 1814–1921
PMG 10 Army Establishment, Compassionate List and Royal Bounty, 1812–1916
PMG 11 Army Establishment, Widows' Pensions, 1810–1920
PMG 12 Ordnance Half Pay, Pensions, etc., 1836–1875
PMG 13 Militia, Yeomanry and Volunteers Allowances, 1793–1927
PMG 14 Army Establishment, Miscellaneous Books, 1720–1861
PMG 33 Army Establishment Warrant Officers Non-Effective Pensions, 1909–1928
PMG 34 Army Establishment Schoolmistresses and Nurses Pensions, 1909–1928
PMG 35 Army Establishment Rewards for Distinguished Services, etc., 1873–1941
PMG 36 Army Establishment Rewards to Warrant Officers for Distinguished or Meritorious Services, 1909–1928
PMG 42 Ministry of Pensions Disability Retired Pay, Gratuities, etc., 1917–1920
PMG 43 Ministry of Pensions, Supplementary Allowances and Special Grants, 1916–1920
PMG 44 Ministry of Pensions, Pensions to relatives of Deceased Officers, 1916–1920
PMG 45 Ministry of Pensions, Widows' Pensions, 1917–1919
PMG 46 Ministry of Pensions Children's Allowances, 1916–1920
PMG 47 Ministry of Pensions, Relatives of Missing Officers, 1915–1920
PMG 57 Army Establishment, Civil Officers, Artificers, etc., Superannuation, 1857–1920

State Paper Office
SP 1   State Papers, Henry VIII, General, Domestic and Foreign, 1509–1547

SP 2   State Papers, Henry VIII, Folios, Domestic and Foreign, 1516–1539
SP 10   State Papers, Domestic, Edward VI, 1547–1553
SP 12   State Papers, Domestic, Elizabeth I, 1558–1603
SP 14   State Papers, Domestic, James I, 1603–1625
SP 16   State Papers, Domestic, Charles I, 1625–1649
SP 17   State Papers, Domestic, Charles I, Cases, 1625–1649
SP 28   State Papers, Domestic, Commonwealth Exchequer, 1642–1660

War Office
WO 10   Muster Books and Pay Lists, Artillery, 1708–1878
WO 11   Muster Books and Pay Lists, Engineers, 1816–1878
WO 12   Muster Books and Pay Lists, General, 1732–1878
WO 13   Muster Books and Pay Lists, Militia and Volunteers, 1780–1878
WO 16   Muster Books and Pay Lists, New Series, 1877–1898
WO 17   Monthly Returns, 1759–1865
WO 22   Royal Hospital Chelsea Pension Returns, 1842–1883 (useful for tracing changes of residence and dates of death of pensioners)
WO 25   Registers, Various, 1660–1938 (out pension records)
WO 31   Memoranda Papers, Commander in Chief, 1793–1870
WO 40   Selected Unnumbered Papers, 1753–1859
WO 42   Returns: Certificates of Birth, etc., 1755–1908 (supplied by officers' widows applying for pensions. Includes wills and other personal papers)
WO 54   Ordnance Office Registers, 1594–1871
WO 64   Manuscript Army Lists, 1702–1823
WO 67   Depot Description Books, 1768–1919 (includes physical descriptions with dates and place of birth, trade, etc.)
WO 68   Militia Records, 1759–1925 (includes registers of marriages, baptisms and births)
WO 69   Artillery Records of Service, 1756–1911 (includes registers of marriages and baptisms)
WO 70   Volunteer and Territorial Records, 1860–1957 (no muster rolls after 1912)
WO 73   Monthly Returns: Distribution of the Army, 1859–1946
WO 76   Returns: Records of Officers' Services, 1755–1954
WO 96   Militia Attestation Papers, 1806–1915
WO 97   Soldiers' Documents, 1760–1913
WO 100 Campaign Medals, 1791–1912
WO 108 South African War: Papers, 1899–1905
WO 116 Royal Hospital, Chelsea, Admission Books, Disability and Royal Artillery, 1715–1913
WO 117 Royal Hospital, Chelsea, Admission Books, Length of Service, 1823–1920
WO 118 Royal Hospital, Kilmainham, Admission Books, 1704–1922
WO 119 Royal Hospital, Kilmainham, Discharge Documents of Pensioners, 1783–1822
WO 121 Royal Hospital, Chelsea, Discharge Documents of Pensioners, 1782–1887
WO 122 Royal Hospital, Chelsea, Foreigners' Regiments, 1816–1817

WO 126   South African War, Local Armed Forces, Enrolment Forms,
         1899–1902
WO 127   South African War, Local Armed Forces, Nominal Rolls, 1899–1902
WO 128   South African War, Imperial Yeomanry, Soldiers' Documents,
         1899–1902
WO 131   Royal Hospital Chelsea, Documents of Soldiers awarded deferred
         Pensions, 1838–1896
WO 143   Duke of York's School and Royal Hibernian School, 1801–1980
WO 156   Registers of Baptisms and Banns of Marriage, 1808–1958 (Registers
         kept at several garrisons in the British Isles and in Palestine)
WO 165–WO 179   War of 1939–1945 War Diaries, various theatres
WO 211   H G Hart Papers, 1838–1875

2 Sailors in the Royal Navy

For men serving before the Restoration (1660), no systematic service records
survive in the PRO. Anything there is will be found among the State Papers
(SP), which are best approached through the series of published *Calendars,*
cited above (p. 39). For the service records of ratings who enlisted after 1891
and officers after the 1880s, you should write to Naval Personnel Records.
For the period 1660–c. 1890, the relevant records are in the PRO. Naval
personnel fell into three categories, commissioned officers (almost invariably
from the gentry and upper classes), warrant officers (professional seamen,
usually of humble birth), and ratings. Commissioned officers first went to sea
as midshipmen.

a Commissioned Officers

These men held their ranks by commission from the Crown, and their
principal task was to bring the ship to battle. They were, in order of rank (but
with variations at different times), Admiral of the Fleet, Admiral, Vice-
Admiral, Rear Admiral, Commodore, Captain, Commander, Lieutenant-
Commander, Lieutenant, Sub-Lieutenant. But, beware, officers are not
always exactly described in non-naval records, and terminology can in any
case be confusing:

A man referred to as 'Captain X' may be:
  1 A post-Captain in rank (1700 onwards).
  2 Holding a Captain's commission (before 1700).
  3 A Commander, holding a command (before 20th century).
  4 A Commander, not holding a command (1827–c. 1900).
  5 A Lieutenant, holding a command (before 20th century).
  6 A Captain, Royal Marines, Royal Marine Artillery or Royal Marine Light
    Infantry.
  7 Master of a merchantman (East India Co. or 20th century).

A man referred to as 'the Captain of the Y'* may be:
  1 A post-Captain.

---

*i.e. a ship; such titles as 'Captain of the Foretop', 'Captain of the Hold', indicate jobs held by
senior petty-officers.

The undermentioned Houses are situate within the Boundaries of the

No. of Schedule	Road, Street, &c., and No. or Name of House	HOUSES In-habited	HOUSES Unin-habited (U.), or Building (B.)	Name and Surname of each Person	Relation to Head of Family	Condition	Age of Males	Age of Females	Rank, Profession, or Occupation	Where Born	Whether Blind, or Deaf-and-Dumb

Parish [or Township] of *Edgbaston* — Municipal Borough of *Birmingham*

Total of Houses... 4 — Total of Males and Females... 11 14

II **Entry in the 1861 Census for Edgbaston, Birmingham** (RG 9/2124)

[No. 2.]

204
Cum....

19/7/16

HIS MAJESTY'S 2 N 73 — Regiment of *Foot*
whereof *Genl. the Genl. Harris* is Colonel.

THESE are to certify, that *William Robinson Private*
in *Capt. Davies* Company, in the Regiment aforesaid, born in the
Parish of *Carlisle* in or near the Town of *Carlisle*
in the County of *Cumberland* was enlisted at the Age of *Eighteen*
Years; and hath served in the said Regiment for the space of
Three Years and *73*
Days, as well as in other Corps, after the Age of Eighteen, according to the following
Statement, but in consequence of *Loss of left Eye from a Gun Shot*
Wound received at Waterloo on the 18th June 1815
is rendered unfit for further Service, and is hereby discharged; having first received
all just Demands of Pay, Clothing, &c. from his Entry into the said Regiment to
the date of this Discharge, as appears by the Receipt on the back hereof.

And to prevent any improper use being made of this Discharge, by its falling into
other Hands, the following is a Description of the said *William Robinson.*
He is about *Twenty One* Years of Age; is *Five* Feet *Seven* Inches in
height, *Brown* Hair, *Grey* Eyes, *Fresh*
Complexion, by Trade a *Tailor*

STATEMENT OF SERVICE.

IN WHAT CORPS.	Period.		Serjeant Major.		Qr. Mast. Serjeant.		Serjeant.		Corporal.		Trumpeter or Drummer.		Private.		Total Service.		Total	
	From	To	Yrs.	Days.	Yrs.	Days.	Yrs.	Days.	Yrs.	Days.	Yrs.	Days.	Yrs.	Days.	Yrs.	Days.	Years.	Days.
73 Regt. 1 Apr. 1813	13 June 1815	..	..	..	..	..	..	..	..	..	..	3	73	5	73	2		
TOTAL..			..	..	..	..	..	..	..	..	..	3	73	5	73	2		

Given under my Hand, and Seal of the Regiment, at *Colchester*
the *13* Day of *June* 1816.

J Owen
Capt. McConvey

III **Discharge document for William Robinson who lost an eye
at Waterloo, 1815** (WO 97/855)

2 A commander, holding a command.
3 A Lieutenant-Commander (1914 onwards) holding a command.
4 A Lieutenant holding a command.
5 Any other rank holding a command.

A man referred to as 'Commander X' may be:
1 A Commander in rank (1794 onwards).
2 A post-Captain (rarely, 17–18th centuries).
3 A Lieutenant in Command (18th century, rarely 19th century).
4 A Lieutenant-Commander (1914 onwards).

A man referred to as 'Commander of the Y' may be:
1 The Captain, of whatever rank (before 20th century).
2 The Commander, i.e. executive officer (1827 onwards).

A man referred to as 'Lieutenant-Commander X' may be:
1 A Lieutenant in command (18–19th centuries).
2 A Lieutenant-Commander (1914 onwards).

A man referred to as 'Lieutenant X' may be:
1 A Lieutenant in rank.
2 Holding a Lieutenant's commission (before 1700).
3 A Lieutenant, Royal Marines, Royal Marine Artillery or Royal Marine Light Infantry.
4 A Sub-Lieutenant R.N.

A man addressed as 'Commodore X' may be:
1 A Commodore R.N., otherwise addressed as 'Captain'.
2 Senior Master of a convoy or merchant fleet, otherwise addressed as 'Captain' or 'Mr.'.

A man addressed as 'Admiral X' may be:
1 An Admiral (of the Red, White or Blue before 1863).
2 A Vice-Admiral (likewise).
3 A Rear-Admiral (likewise).
4 A 'Yellow Admiral' of any of the above ranks; i.e. an officer promoted on half pay or after retirement to a rank never exercised except for purposes of pay and pension.

An outline of an officer's career can usually be constructed from the various printed and typescript compilations available, such as the *Navy List* and naval biographies. You should then try looking at the Lieutenant's Passing Certificates (1691–1902) (ADM 6, ADM 13, ADM 107 and a few in ADM1/5123), which give information on the candidate's previous career; and the Records and Returns of Officer's Services (ADM 9, ADM 10, ADM 196). Once you know the name of the ship on which a man served, the Captains' Logs (ADM 51) may be useful; Lieutenants' Logs are held by the National Maritime Museum. You may also find references to an officer in the

Indexes (ADM 12) to the Admiralty Correspondence (ADM 1), although, obviously, the higher a man was in rank the more likely is this to be the case.

Officer's marriage certificates may be found among the Supplementary Papers from 1861 (ADM 13). The volumes have integral indexes.

b Warrant Officers

Warrant officers had authority in their own departments by virtue of a warrant from the Navy Board, Sick and Hurt Board or Ordnance Board, usually as the result of an examination. They included such men as the master (responsible for navigating the ship, under the captain's orders), boatswain, gunner, engineer, carpenter, surgeon, chaplain, some sailmakers and some coopers.

The best place to start looking for records of warrant officers is among their records of service (ADM 29, ADM 104), which give brief details of all men superannuated after 1802, and who therefore started their careers well back into the eighteenth century. There are some warrant officers mentioned in the records of officer's services (ADM 196), in the Seniority Lists (ADM 118) and the Warrant Books (ADM 6, ADM 11). Censuses were sometimes taken of some types of warrant officer (ADM 6, ADM 11), and almost all of them had to take some kind of examination which resulted in registers of their certificates of competency (ADM 6, ADM 13, ADM 106). Masters and surgeons also kept logs (ADM 52, ADM 101); the latter sometimes contain vivid accounts of places visited. There are references to chaplains in Chatham Chest records (ADM 82), Full Pay Ledgers (ADM 24), and Accountant General Registers (ADM 30). Some more recent records of chaplains are still held by the Chaplain of the Fleet.

c Ratings

For the service records of a rating before 1853, you will be in difficulty unless you know the name of the ship on which the man served at a particular time. If you do not, but think that your ancestor was involved in a specific battle, then you could try the Medal Rolls (ADM 171) which are arranged by campaign. If you know where a man was serving at a given time, but not in which ship, you can find out which ships were there at the date in question by looking at the List Books (ADM 8).

If the name of the ship is known the Ships' Musters (from 1667) (ADM 36–ADM 39) can be used, and by working through preceding and succeeding musters a more or less complete record of service established. You may find the man's age and place of birth in the muster, and if a Description Book survives with the Muster you will find many more personal details. If there is no muster, the Ships' Pay Books (ADM 31–ADM 35) will at least confirm a man's presence on board. You will find the full record of service of a rating superannuated after 1802 in the Warrant Officers' and Seamen's Services (ADM 29).

In 1853, Continuous Service Engagement was introduced, and ratings were assigned Continuous Service (CS) numbers. When a man entered the service, a certificate was completed giving his date and place of birth, description and ship, and brief records of his subsequent service were latter added. This system ended in 1872 and was replaced by new Official Numbers, which referred to the records of Seamen's Services. These two series up to 1891 are at the PRO (ADM 139, ADM 188), but thereafter it only holds records of ratings serving with armoured cars in Russia from 1915 to 1917 (ADM 116/1717).

d Sea Fencibles
Sea Fencibles were the naval equivalent of the Militia: forces raised for local defensive service only. There are pay lists for the period 1798–1810 (ADM 28).

e Coastguards
Coastguard service records, 1816–1923 (ADM 175), and Muster Books, 1824–1857 (ADM 119), are among the Admiralty records, and there are pension papers in the Paymaster General's records (PMG 23, PMG 70). An index of coastguards is in preparation; apply to Mrs Stage.

f Other sources: Pensions, Wills, etc.
Ledgers recordings Full and Half Pay of officers (ADM 22, ADM 24, PMG 15), pensions of officers and men, and widows' pensions may be used to supplement the sources above, though they rarely record genealogical information except in any explanatory note of a first or last payment. If you can find no other means of establishing a date of death, you may at least learn an approximate date.

To identify any relevant pension records it is necessary to know the reason for which the pension was awarded: wounds, disability, meritorious conduct, poverty, widow's pension, etc. Payments are recorded in many places. There are some for the years 1654–1660 in the Admiralty Accounting Departments' Bill Books (ADM 18), and others for wounded men in the Chatham Chest Records (ADM 82). The majority of pensions were paid by Greenwich Hospital, which were recorded in the various registers of that institution (ADM 73, ADM 165, ADM 166, PMG 15, PMG 16, PMG 18–PMG 20, PMG 23–PMG 25, PMG 56, PMG 69–PMG 72). From 1822 to 1912 (by the Statute 46 and 47 Vict., c. 32) Greenwich Hospital pensions included payments to the widows and children of warrant officers, petty officers, and ratings who died in service but not in action (ADM 166). In 1916 responsibility for payments under the Act passed to the Ministry of Pensions, whose records are with those of the Paymaster General (PMG 42–PMG 47).

Where papers survive in support of applications for a pension or bounty they can be valuable genealogical sources. The applications of widows' pensions (ADM 6, ADM 22) for instance, include marriage certificates, and give the date of the husband's death. You may also find material of use in the In-Letters (ADM 65), Admission Papers (ADM 73) and papers on widows' charities (ADM 6, ADM 68) of Greenwich Hospital. The Navy Board Bounty Papers (ADM 106) are petitions from poor widows, orphans and mothers of officers and men killed or mortally wounded at sea. They often give precise details of the death, and are supported by parochial certificates of marriage, baptism or kinship as appropriate.

There is a large number of seamen's wills among the Admiralty records (ADM 48), as well as among the records of the Prerogative Court of Canterbury (see III/3 above). After 1815, if a seaman died with wages totalling less than £20 owing to him, his will was not eligible for proving in the PCC, so you should look for it in the records of the appropriate local court. Besides the original wills, there are copies of wills and original letters of administration (1800–1860) among the Seamen's, Officers' and Civilians' Effects Papers (ADM 44, ADM 45). These records are more complete than the series of wills, and are particularly useful for the genealogist as you will often find birth and marriage certificates attached to the grant.

g Medals
Citations of awards appear in the *London Gazette*. Information is also available from the Ministry of Defence.

For prisoners of war see IV/24 below.
For Poles serving in British Navy in Second World War see page 37.

Bibliography

Books

J Campbell and W Stevenson, *Lives of the British Admirals* (London, 1917)
J Charnock, *Biographia Navalis* (London, 1794–1798)
Dictionary of National Biography
K Douglas-Morris, *The Naval General Service Medal, 1793–1840* (Margate, 1982)
J Marshall, *Royal Naval Biography* (London, 1823–1830)
W R O'Byrne, *A Naval Biographical Dictionary* (London, 1849)

Published Finding Aids

Calendar of State Papers, Domestic Series (London, 1856–1972)
Commissioned Sea Officers of the Royal Navy, 1660–1815 (London, 1954)
A G Kealy, *Chaplains of the Royal Navy, 1626–1903* (Portsmouth, 1905)
List of Sea Officers (London, 1800–1824)
The Navy List (London, annually from 1814)
D Steel, *Navy List* (London, 1782–1817)
London Gazette (1665 to date)

Unpublished Finding Aids

Card index of seamen's wills (ADM 48), A–H only
E H B Fairbrother, Index of Chaplains, MS
Index of lieutenants' passing certificates, 1789–1818 (ADM 107), TS
Interim notes on means of reference to ADM 196
A G Kealy, List of Chaplains, Royal Navy, 1626–1816

Records

Admiralty

ADM 1	Admiralty and Secretariat Papers, 1660–1969 (index in ADM 12)
ADM 6	Admiralty and Secretariat, Various Registers, Returns and Certificates, 1673–1960
ADM 8	List Books, 1673–1909
ADM 9	Original Returns of Officers' Services, 1817–1848 (index in ADM 10)
ADM 10	Indexes and Compilations, Series I (includes index to ADM 9), 1660–1851
ADM 11	Indexes and Compilations, Series II (includes commissioned and warrant officers' records), 1741–1869
ADM 12	Indexes and Compilations, Series III (includes digests and indexes to ADM 1 and ADM 16), 1660–1938
ADM 13	Supplementary Papers, 1803–1917
ADM 18	Accounting Departments' Bill Books, 1642–1831
ADM 22	Registers of Salaries and Pensions, 1734–1934
ADM 24	Officers' Full Pay Registers, 1795–1872
ADM 28	Sea Fencibles Pay Lists, 1798–1810
ADM 29	Registers of Warrant Officers' and Seamen's Services, 1802–1919
ADM 30	Accounting Departments' Registers, 1689–1836
ADM 31	Ships' Pay Books: Controller's, 1691–1710
ADM 32	Ships' Pay Books: Ticket Office, 1692–1856
ADM 33	Ships' Pay Books: Treasurer's, Series I, 1669–1778
ADM 34	Ships' Pay Books: Treasurer's, Series II, 1766–1785
ADM 35	Ships' Pay Books: Treasurer's, Series III, 1777–1832
ADM 36	Ships' Musters, Series, I, 1688–1808
ADM 37	Ships' Musters, Series II, 1804–1842
ADM 38	Ships' Musters, Series III, 1793–1878
ADM 39	Ships' Musters, Series IV, 1667–1798
ADM 44	Seamen's Effects Papers, 1800–1860 (alphabetically arranged)
ADM 45	Officers' and Civilians' Effects Papers, 1830–1860 (alphabetically arranged)
ADM 48	Seamen's Wills, 1786–1882 (index in ADM 142)
ADM 50	Admirals' Journals, 1702–1916
ADM 51	Captains' Logs, 1669–1852
ADM 52	Masters' Logs, 1672–1840
ADM 65	Greenwich Hospital In-Letters, 1702–1869
ADM 68	Greenwich Hospital Accounts, 1696–1865
ADM 73	Greenwich Hospital Miscellaneous Registers, 1704–1966
ADM 82	Chatham Chest, 1617–1807
ADM 101	Medical Journals, 1785–1880
ADM 104	Medical Departments' Registers, 1774–1939
ADM 106	Navy Board Records, 1659–1837
ADM 107	Navy Board Passing Certificates, 1691–1848
ADM 116	Admiralty and Secretariat Cases, 1852–1960 (index in ADM 12)
ADM 118	Seniority Lists, 1717–1850
ADM 119	Ships' Musters: Coastguard and Revenue Cruisers, 1824–1857
ADM 139	Accounting Departments: Continuous Service Engagement Books, 1853–1872

ADM 141 Registers of Seamen's Effects Papers, 1802–1861
ADM 142 Registers of Seamen's Wills (index to ADM 48), 1786–1909
ADM 165 Greenwich Hospital Registers of Pensions to Naval and Marine Officers and Greenwich Hospital Staff, 1871–1961
ADM 166 Greenwich Hospital Registers of Pensions to Widows of Seamen and Marines, 1882–1949
ADM 171 Medal Rolls, 1793–1914
ADM 175 Coastguard Records of Service, 1816–1947
ADM 188 Registers of Seamen's Services, 1873–1895*
ADM 196 Records of Officers' Services, 1777–1954
ADM 240 Royal Naval Reserve: Records of Officers' Services, 1862–1960

Paymaster General's Office
PMG 15 Naval Establishment, Half Pay, Retired Pay and Unattached Pay, 1836–1920
PMG 16 Naval Establishment, Pensions for Miscellaneous Services, Wounds, Widows, etc., 1836–1920
PMG 18 Naval Establishment, Compassionate List, 1837–1921
PMG 19 Pensions for Widows of Naval Officers, 1836–1929
PMG 20 Pensions for Widows of Marine Officers and Relatives of Naval and Marine Officers, killed on duty, 1870–1919
PMG 23 Coastguard: Civil Pensions, 1855–1935
PMG 24 Salaried Officers' Civil Pensions, 1836–1918
PMG 25 Artificers' and Labourers' Civil Pensions, 1836–1928
PMG 42 War of 1914–1918, Ministry of Pensions, Disability Retired Pay, Gratuities, etc., 1917–1920
PMG 43 War of 1914–1918, Ministry of Pensions, Supplementary Allowances and Special Grants, 1916–1920
PMG 44 War of 1914–1918, Ministry of Pensions, Pensions to Relatives of Deceased Officers, 1916–1920
PMG 45 War of 1914–1918, Ministry of Pensions, Widows' Pensions, 1916–1919
PMG 46 War of 1914–1918, Ministry of Pensions, Children's Allowances, 1916–1920
PMG 47 War of 1914–1918, Ministry of Pensions, Relatives of Missing Officers, 1915–1920
PMG 56 Naval Establishment, Warlike Operations, Pensions, etc., 1914–1928
PMG 69 Engineers, Subordinate and Warrant Officers, etc., Pensions, 1874–1924
PMG 70 Greenwich Hospital Pensions and Civil Superannuation Allowances, 1866–1928
PMG 71 Naval Pensions, 1846–1921
PMG 72 Widows and Dependents of Seamen and Marines, Pensions, 1921–1926

SP State Paper Office

---

*This includes full service records for anyone who enlisted pre or during 1891.

3 Royal Marines

Soldiers were recruited exclusively for sea service from 1690. Until 1755, control of marine regiments was committed to military or naval authorities, depending on whether the men were on shore or at sea. The records of the Marines are thus divided among the papers of the Admiralty (ADM), State Paper Office (SP) and War Office (WO) during this period.

On 3 April 1755 an Order in Council approved the raising of 5000 Marines, who were grouped in 50 'companies', each of which was assigned to one of three 'Grand Divisions', quartered respectively at Chatham, Plymouth and Portsmouth, under the control of the Board of Admiralty. The number of companies steadily grew and the Marines were never again disbanded. They were designated 'Royal' Marines by George III in an order dated 29 April 1802. From 1805 to 1869 there was a further Division, quartered at Woolwich. In 1848 the Portsmouth Division moved to Forton barracks, Gosport, and in 1861 a depot was established at Walmer, Kent (later the Royal Marine Depot, Deal). The 'companies' within each division were purely administrative units, which bore no relation to the tactical units formed when the Marines were on active service. These tactical units might contain men of many separate divisions.

In 1804 separate companies of artillery were authorised (again by Order in Council), each to be attached to one of the existing divisions. (Before this date men from the Royal Artillery had been called on to serve at sea when required). The total number of artillery companies rose and fell according to demand: for a time in the 1830s, for example, there were only two such companies, both attached to the Portsmouth Division. The whole corps was named the Royal Marine Light Infantry from 1855, but in 1859 the Royal Marine Artillery was formed into a separate Division for which Eastney barracks was built. In 1923 the RMLI ('Red Marines') and RMA ('Blue Marines') were merged into a single corps of Royal Marines.

a Officers
No records of officers' services for men appointed before 1793 have survived, although confirmation of a commission or appointment may sometimes be found. For officers commissioned after 1793 you should look first in the Records of Officers' Services (ADM 196), which give full details of service, and sometimes also include the name and profession of the officer's father. These records, however, are still incomplete until about 1837, as officers who served only for a short period into the nineteenth century are not recorded. These volumes are open to public inspection 30 years after the last discharge date of an officer in a volume. The volumes for officers appointed after 1906 have final dates which fall within this closure period, so records are only available of officers appointed before 1906. Enquiries about officers appointed later should be set to the Commandant General of the Royal Marines.

Where no full record of service survives, you may learn something from the Lists of Marine Officers, two incomplete sets of which are among the

Seniority Lists (ADM 118) and the Lists of Officers (ADM 192). The *Navy Lists* also include Marine officers. Some further information may occasionally be gleaned from the Commission and Subsistence Books (ADM 96) among the Marine Pay Office Registers, but the Commissions and Appointments (ADM 6) contain no helpful details for genealogists. In 1822 a survey was made of half pay officers, which give their age and little else (ADM 6/409).

Separate records of warrant officers have survived only in one volume among the other records of Officers' Services (ADM 196/67). If the officer you are looking for is not there, your best chance is that he became a commissioned officer later.

b Other Ranks
Records of service for other ranks survive in abundance, but you may find it difficult to trace an individual unless you know his division or company. There was no central system of numbering Marines until 1884, so until then men of the same name can be differentiated only by their company number. The records are mainly arranged by divisions, but if you know your ancestor's company you can ascertain his division from tables in the Lists of Officers. If you cannot determine his division, you will have to search through the records of each in turn. Men normally remained with the company in which they enlisted unless promoted, when they were sometimes transferred.

There is a series of various registers, known collectively as Description Books (ADM 158), which may be helpful. They are arranged by date of attestation (i.e. enlistment) and by the initial letter of the man's surname, and give age, parish of birth and a physical description, but not the ships or battalions in which a man served. They cover several years in each volume, and an individual may be in more than one book, so they can be useful if you know only a man's name. If you know the date of a man's discharge, you may do better to start with the Attestation Forms (ADM 157) which were completed when a man enlisted, but until 1883 were filed by the discharge date, and arranged by divisions and initial letters. You should find on these forms some notes on service, and perhaps the date and circumstances of death.

In 1884 each man was given his own distinctive number, and Records of Service were introduced (ADM 159). You will have a long search if you do not know a man's number as there is no key and they are only roughly chronological by date of enlistment. The information provided once you have found your man is extensive: date and place of birth, trade, religion, date and place of enlistment, physical description, a full record of service, and comments on conduct, promotions etc. The records in the PRO cover men enlisted up to 1901; for men enlisted after that date you should write to the Royal Marines' Drafting and Record Office.

You may find that a look in the Effective and Subsistence Lists (ADM 96) is helpful in providing hints for other places to search. They contain no personal details but list men for pay and expenses and may indicate, for example, that a man served abroad. If you know that a man served on a particular ship and

IV Sketch of a forest official from a roll of forest proceedings relating to the Forest of Dean. Late thirteenth century (E 32/31)

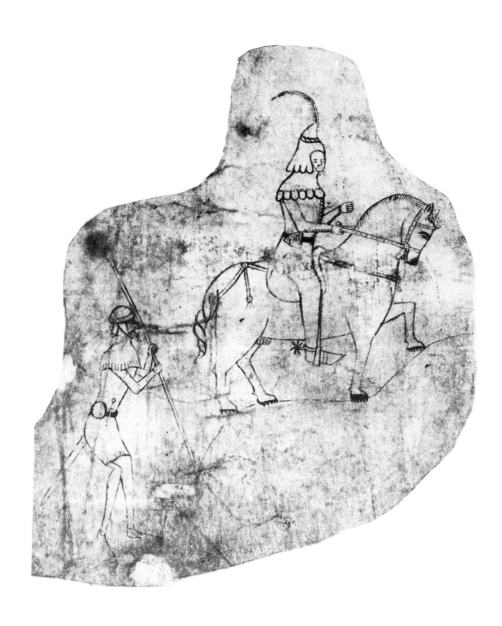

**V Drawing of a King's Messenger with a footman,
from an account of messengers' expenses.
Fourteenth century** (E 101/309/11)

when, you should consult the Ship's Musters (ADM 36–ADM 39), and if you think he may have been decorated you could look in the Medal Rolls (ADM 171). For the Second World War there are War Diaries (ADM 202), arranged by unit, ship or operation; for commando units a look in the Combined Operations Headquarters records may be worthwhile (DEFE 2).

c Other Records

i Divisions
There are some records of the various divisions in the PRO, which include such useful genealogical materials as registers of births, marriages and deaths and discharge and embarkation books, as well as correspondence (ADM 81, ADM 183–ADM 185, ADM 193).

ii Courts Martial
Registers of Courts Martial survive for the Portsmouth Division from 1834 and for the Plymouth Division from 1836, together with those for certain units serving overseas (ADM 194). Some earlier papers will be found with those of Royal Naval trials (ADM 13). These records are closed for a period of 75 years after the date of the last entry in the volume.

iii Pensions
These are to be found among the Royal Naval pensions, with the records of Greenwich Hospital and the Paymaster General (see IV/2 above).

iv Central Records
There are separate sections among the Admiralty In- (ADM 1) and Out-letters (ADM 2) for correspondence and papers on policy matters, including recruitment and deployment, concerning the Marines. You will also find correspondence of the Marine Pay Office (ADM 96) until 1862, although it became part of the office of the Accountant General of the Navy in 1831 (which in turn became part of the Paymaster General's Office in 1835).

The Royal Marine Office, now the Commandant General's Office, kept letter books, first general (ADM 56), then from 1868 classified by correspondent: divisions (ADM 57–ADM 63), Admiralty (ADM 191), War Office (ADM 200). There are also some records of the Office among the General Standing Orders (ADM 64).

Bibliography

Books

H E Blumberg, *Britain's Sea Soldiers, 1914–1919* (Devonport, 1927)
C Field, *Britain's Sea Soldiers* (Liverpool, 1924)
E Fraser and L G Carr-Laughton, *Royal Marine Artillery* (London, 1930)
A C Hampshire, *The Royal Marines' Tercentenary* (London, 1964)
R B Lockhart, *The Marines were there* (London, 1950)
J L Moulton, *The Royal Marines* (London, 1973)
P C Smith, *Per Mare Per Terram* (St Ives, Hunts, 1974)

Published Finding Aids

Alphabetical Guide to the War Office and other materials, PRO Lists and
Indexes, vol. LIII (1931)
Navy List (London, annually from 1814)

Records

See list under Royal Navy, above IV/2

Admiralty
ADM 2   Admiralty and Secretariat, Out Letters, 1659–1859
ADM 6   Admiralty and Secretariat, Various Registers, Returns and
          Certificates, 1673–1960 (including registers of baptisms, marriages
          and burials in the Royal Marine Churches on the Isle of Sheppey)
ADM 56   Royal Marine Office, Letter Books: General, 1806–1868
ADM 57   Royal Marine Office, Letter Books: Woolwich, 1868–1869
ADM 58   Royal Marine Office, Letter Books: Chatham, 1868–1884
ADM 59   Royal Marine Office, Letter Books: Royal Marine Artillery,
          1868–1884
ADM 60   Royal Marine Office, Letter Books: Gosport, 1868–1884
ADM 61   Royal Marine Office, Letter Books: Plymouth, 1868–1884
ADM 62   Royal Marine Office, Letter Books: Deal, 1868–1884
ADM 63   Royal Marine Office, Letter Books: Miscellaneous, 1834–1889
ADM 64   Royal Marines, General Standing Orders, 1888–1936
ADM 81   Royal Marines, Woolwich Division, 1805–1869
ADM 96   Marine Pay Office, 1688–1862
ADM 157   Royal Marines, Attestation Forms, 1790–1901
ADM 158   Royal Marines, Description Books, c. 1750–1940 (1889–1940,
          Deal Depot only)
ADM 159   Royal Marines, Registers of Service, 1842–1905
ADM 183   Royal Marines, Chatham Division, 1755–1941
ADM 184   Royal Marines, Plymouth Division, 1760–1941
ADM 185   Royal Marines, Portsmouth Division, 1763–1941
ADM 191   Royal Marine Office, Letter Books: Admiralty, 1826–1884
ADM 192   Royal Marines, Lists of Officers, 1760–1886
ADM 193   Royal Marines, Miscellaneous, 1761–1918
ADM 194   Courts Martial Registers, 1812–1916
ADM 200   Royal Marines Office, Letter Books: War Office, 1868–1884
ADM 201   Royal Marine Office, Correspondence and Papers, 1761–1928
ADM 202   Royal Marines, War Diaries, 1939–1946

Ministry of Defence
DEFE 2   Combined Operations Headquarters Records, 1937–1951

War Office
WO 1   In Letters, 1732–1868
WO 3   Out Letters, Commander in Chief, 1765–1868
WO 4   Out Letters, Secretary at War, 1684–1861
WO 6   Out Letters, Secretary of State, 1793–1859
WO 26   Miscellany Books, 1670–1817

WO 32   Registered Papers, General, 1853–1977
WO 33   Reports and Miscellaneous Papers, 1853–1948
WO 44   Ordnance Office, In Letters, 1682–1873
WO 47   Ordnance Office, Minutes, 1644–1856
WO 81   Judge Advocate General's Office, Letter Books, 1715–1900

4 Royal Air Force and Royal Flying Corps

The PRO holds no RAF personnel records. The Air Ministry group of records consist of central office papers and operational records, which often include the names of men and women serving but it would be a long job to find any particular person. Personnel records of all RAF ranks will be released to relatives only on application to RAF Personnel Management. Other records such as notification of casualties, and honours are held by RAF Officers' Records.

You will find some officers' pensions among the Paymaster General's records for the period 1916–1920 (PMG 42, PMG 44), and information on prisoners of war among Air Ministry and Foreign Office files (AIR 40, AIR 46, AIR 49, FO 916). It may also be worth looking at the RAF monographs and narratives (AIR 41), and the citations and grants of commissions and honours (AIR 2, AIR 30). For Poles serving in the RAF during Second World War see page 37.

Published Finding Aids
Air Force List (from 1918)

Unpublished Finding Aids

Air Records as Sources for Biography and Genealogy, PRO leaflet no. 46

Records

Air Ministry
AIR 1/819 and AIR 10/232–237 Muster list of all RAF personnel on 1 April 1918
AIR 2   Correspondence, 1887–1980
AIR 20/2336   List of all aircrew held prisoner by the Germans in late 1944
AIR 30   Submission Papers, 1918–1955
AIR 40   Directorate of Intelligence and other Intelligence Papers, 1923–1958
AIR 41   Air Historical Branch, Monographs and Narratives, 1942–1950
AIR 46   Air Missions, 1939–1960
AIR 49   History of RAF Medical Services, Narratives and Drafts, 1919–1951

Foreign Office
FO 916   War of 1939–1945, Consular (War) Department: Prisoners of War and Internees, 1940–1946

Paymaster General's Office
PMG 42   War of 1914–1918, Ministry of Pensions, Disability Retired Pay, Gratuities, etc., 1916–1920
PMG 44   War of 1914–1918, Ministry of Pensions, Pensions to Relatives of Deceased Officers, 1916–1920

5 Royal Irish Constabulary

This peace keeping force was, in effect, created in 1836 when the local groups of sub constables were united under the command of an Inspector-General. This force was given the title Royal Irish Constabulary in 1867. It was responsible for the whole of Ireland with the exception of Dublin, and so was disbanded in August 1922.

The main series of service records for members of the Royal Irish Constabulary is among the Home Office papers (HO 184). The registers are arranged by service number, but there are separate alphabetical indexes. They normally give name, age, height, religious affiliation, native county, trade, marital status, native county of wife (but not her name), date of appointment, counties in which the man served, length of service and date of retirement or death, but no information about parentage.

Pensions and allowances granted to officers, men and staff, and to their widows and children are recorded among the Paymaster General's records (PMG 48), and usually give the recipient's address. There are also registers of deceased pensioners (1877–1918) and of awards of pension made on the disbandment of the force in this class. Among the Colonial Office records are files on pension options at the time of disbandment, arranged by county (CO 904/175–6).

For the earlier force a list of superannuations awarded was published by order of Parliament in 1832, giving names, period of service, amount granted, and the nature of the injury which was the cause of the superannuation.

There are more records relating to the activities of the Irish police, but although there are references among them to individual officers you have no way of finding them short of reading through great numbers of files (CO 903, CO 906, HO 45, HO 100, T 1, T 160–T 164, T 192).

Bibliography

Published Finding Aids

House of Commons Sessional Papers, 1831–1832, vol. XXVI, p. 465 (List of superannuations)

Records

Colonial Office
CO 903   Ireland, Confidential Print, 1885–1919
CO 904   Dublin Castle Records, 1795–1926
CO 906   Irish Office, 1796–1924

Home Office
HO 45   Registered Papers, 1839–1950
HO 100   Ireland, Correspondence and Papers, 1782–1851
HO 184   Royal Irish Constabulary, 1816–1922

Paymaster General's Office
PMG 48   Royal Irish Constabulary, Pensions, 1873-1925

Treasury
T 1   Treasury Board Papers, 1557-1920
T 160   Finance Files, 1887-1948
T 161   Supply Files, 1905-1961
T 162   Establishment Files, 1890-1948
T 163   General Files, 1888-1948
T 164   Pensions (Superannuation Files), 1893-1970
T 192   Ireland Files, 1920-1922

6 Merchant Seamen

There is a wealth of material documenting English, Welsh, Scottish and Irish merchant seamen in the PRO, but it relates mainly to the years 1835 to 1857. There is little from before this period, and after 1857 the surviving records have become scattered.

a Seamen's Registers, 1835-1857
The Merchant Shipping Act of 1835 provided for the registration of seamen. The resulting registers give the name of the seaman, his age, place of birth, rank and the name of his ship, and from 1844 such additional details as a physical description and his service record. Errors in transcription are frequent in the early registers, as many of the entries were made from the scrawled signature of illiterates. It was, moreover, not uncommon for a seaman to give a false name.

The registers are in four separate series, which overlap to some extent and represent different systems of registration. The first series (BT 120) consists simply of alphabetically arranged entries, while the second (BT 119) is roughly alphabetical with an index and cross references to the Crew Lists (see below). A ticket system was introduced in 1845, which lasted until 1853, and the register (BT 113) gives full genealogical details as well as a physical description and a man's service record. The last series (BT 116) after the ticket system was abolished, lists seamen alphabetically, giving age, place of birth, and details of the voyage.

b Muster Rolls, Agreements and Crew Lists

i 1747-1834
A few muster rolls survive for some ports, arranged by year and port, but without indexes (BT 98).

ii 1835-1844
In 1835, Crew Lists replaced the Muster Rolls, and the registers (above) are the means of reference to them. You will need to look first, therefore, in the Register where you will find the number of the port and the name of the ship. Each port was assigned its own number (there is a key in the class list) and the Crew Lists are arranged by those numbers and by year. There are

also Port Rotation Numbers, but there is no longer a key to them so they should be ignored. The Crew Lists (BT 98) should tell you a man's name, age, place of birth, quality (i.e. rank), the ship in which he last served, the date and place of his joining, the time and place of his death or of leaving the ship, and how he was disposed of.

iii 1845–1856
The information in the Crew Lists (BT 98) for these years is like that for the previous period, but the task of locating an entry is much more complicated. Reference is again from the Seamen's Registers (above) but the ship's name is not quoted. C T and M J Watts in their article give a sample entry to illustrate the procedures, for one James Watts in 1846 (BT 113/24):

Out	Home
1140–75–2	1140–75–2
75–6–4	64–31–7

This means that Watts was on a Newcastle registered vessel (75 in the top line), which left Newcastle (75 on the bottom line under 'Out'), on 6 April 1846 (6–4 on the bottom line). He left the ship in London (64 in bottom line under 'Home') on 31 July 1846. The Crew Lists for this period are listed by port and year and, as the ship's name is not known, you must be prepared to search through all the boxes for the appropriate port and year; there may be as many as thirty.

iv 1857–1860
In 1857 the system changed again, and the Crew Lists (BT 98) are arranged thereafter by year and numerically by ship's number. Each ship has a unique number, which can be found in the *Mercantile Navy List*.

v 1861–1938
The PRO holds only a 10% sample of Crew Lists after 1861 (BT 99, BT 100, BT 144, BT 165). The largest single collection of them is now held by the Memorial University of Newfoundland (c. 70%), to which there is a microfiche index in the PRO. A small selection of lists for the period 1861–1913 has been deposited locally, and there is a list of these places of deposit in the class list. The National Maritime Museum has the 90% not held by the PRO for the years 1861, 1862, 1865, 1875, 1885, 1895 and 1905.

c Certificates of Competency and Service: Masters, Mates and Engineers
By an order of 1845, the Board of Trade authorised a system of voluntary examinations of competency for men intending to become masters or mates of foreign going and home trade British merchant ships (BT 122–BT 127). These gradually became compulsory. From 1862 there are also certificates for engineers (BT 139–BT 142), and for skippers and mates of fishing boats from 1883 (BT 129, BT 130, BT 138). Colonial certificates were entered separately (BT 128). You should find in the certificates name, place and date of birth, date and place of issue of the certificate and rank examined or served in. Deaths, injuries and retirements have also been noted down.

For masters only the Lloyd's series of Captains' Registers duplicates the information in the Registers of Certificates of Competency and provide supplementary information. They are kept in the Guildhall Library; entries are in alphabetical order.

d Apprentices
An index was formed of all indentured apprentices under the Merchant Shipping Act of 1835, and is now in the PRO (BT 150). In addition, five yearly specimens of the copy indentures of apprentices on merchant vessels and on fishing vessels have been preserved (BT 151, BT 152).

e Births, Deaths and Marriages
By the Seamen's Fund Winding-up Act, 1851, the masters of British ships were required to hand over the wages and effects of any seaman who had died during a voyage. Registers (BT 153) were maintained and provide useful information: the name, Register Ticket number, date of engagement, and the place, date and cause of the man's death, with the name and port of his ship, the master's name, the date and place of payment of wages, the amount of wages and the date they were sent to the Board of Trade. The indexes to these registers (BT 154, BT 155), by seamen and by ship, give simple page references. Associated with the registers are printed monthly lists of dead seamen (BT 156) giving name and age, rating, nationality or birthplace, last address, and cause and place of death. There are also nine manuscript registers (BT 157), containing half yearly lists of deaths, classified by cause.

Following the Merchant Shipping Act of 1854, registers were compiled from the official logs, of births, marriages and deaths at sea. All three are recorded from 1854 to 1883, births and deaths only from 1883 to 1887, and deaths only from 1888 (BT 158). Masters were further required by the Registration of Births and Deaths Act, 1874, to report births and deaths on board ships to the Registrar General of Shipping and Seamen, where they were entered in two separate registers (BT 159, BT 160).

For further biographical information on ordinary seamen after 1870 and on officers after 1913, you should write to the Registrar General of Shipping and Seamen.

Bibliography

Books

N G Cox, 'The Records of the Registrar General of Shipping and Seamen', *Maritime History*, vol. II (1972), pp. 168–188.
K Matthews, 'Crew Lists, Agreements and Official Logs of the British Empire 1863–1913, now in the possession of the Maritime History Group, Memorial University, Newfoundland', *Business History*, vol. XVI (1974), pp. 78–80
C T and M J Watts, 'Unravelling Merchant Seamen's Records', *Genealogists' Magazine*, vol. XIX (1979), pp. 313–321

Published Finding Aids

Index to the Crew Lists, Agreements and Official Logs at the Memorial University of Newfoundland, microfiche
Mercantile Navy List (London, annually from 1857)

Unpublished Finding Aids

Records of the Registrar General of Shipping and Seamen, PRO leaflet no. 8

Records

Board of Trade: Registrar General of Shipping and Seamen
BT 98   Agreements and Crew Lists, Series I, 1747–1860
BT 99   Agreements and Crew Lists, Series II, 1861–1938
BT 100   Agreements and Crew Lists, Series III, 1835–1954
BT 112   Register of Seamen, Series II, 1835–1844 (index in BT 119)
BT 113   Register of Seamen's Tickets, 1845–1854 (index in BT 114)
BT 114   Alphabetical Register of Seamen's Tickets, 1845–1854 (index to BT 113)
BT 115   Alphabetical Register of Masters, 1845–1854
BT 116   Register of Seamen, Series III, 1853–1857
BT 119   Alphabetical List of Seamen, 1835–1844 (index to BT 112)
BT 120   Register of Seamen, Series I, 1835–1836
BT 122   Registers of Certificates of Competency, Masters and Mates, Foreign Trade, 1845–1900 (index in BT 127)
BT 123   Registers of Certificates of Competency, Masters and Mates of Steamships, 1881–1895 (index in BT 127)
BT 124   Registers of Certificates of Service, Masters and Mates, Foreign Trade, 1850–1888 (index in BT 127)
BT 125   Registers of Certificates of Competency, Masters and Mates, Home Trade, 1854–1888 (index in BT 127)
BT 126   Registers of Certificates of Service, Masters and Mates, Home Trade, 1854–1888 (index in BT 127)
BT 127   Indexes to registers of Competency and Service, Masters and Mates, Foreign and Home Trade, 1845–1894 (BT 122–BT 126)
BT 128   Registers of Certificates of Competency, Masters and Mates, Colonial Trade, 1871–1921
BT 129   Registers of Certificates of Competency, Skippers, Mates, etc. of Fishing Boats, 1880–1898 (index in BT 138)
BT 130   Registers of Certificates of Service, Skippers, Mates, etc. of Fishing Boats, 1883–1917 (index in BT 138)
BT 138   Indexes to Registers of Competency and Service, Skippers, Mates, etc. of Fishing Boats, 1880–1917 (BT 129, BT 130)
BT 139   Registers of Certificates of Competency, Engineers, 1861–1907 (index in BT 141)
BT 140   Registers of Certificates of Competency, Engineers (Colonial), 1862–1921 (index in BT 141)
BT 141   Indexes to Registers of Certificates of Competency, Engineers, 1861–1921 (BT 139, BT 140)

BT 142 Registers of Certificates of Service, Engineers, 1862-1921
BT 143 Registers of Certificates of Competency and Service, Miscellaneous, 1845-1849
BT 144 Agreements and Crew Lists, Series IV, Fishing Agreements, 1884-1929
BT 150 Index of Apprentices, 1824-1953
BT 151 Apprentices' Indentures, 1845-1950
BT 152 Apprentices' Indentures for Fishing, 1895-1935
BT 153 Registers of Wages and Effects of Deceased Seamen, 1852-1889 (index in BT 154, BT 155)
BT 154 Indexes to Names of Seamen, 1855-1889 (BT 153)
BT 155 Indexes to Names of Ships, 1855-1889 (BT 153)
BT 156 Monthly lists of Deaths of Seamen, 1886-1890
BT 157 Registers of Seamen's Deaths, Classified by Cause, 1882-1888
BT 158 Registers of Births, Deaths and Marriages of Passengers at sea, 1854-1890
BT 159 Registers of Deaths at Sea of British Nationals, 1875-1888
BT 160 Registers of Births at Sea of British Nationals, 1875-1891
BT 165 Ships' Official Logs, 1902-1919

7 Crown Employees and Civil Servants

There are numerous places among the Public Records to look for material relating to Crown and Public Servants, most notably among the records of the relevant departments of state and the records of the Treasury, but also in other less obvious classes. It would however, be impractical to attempt to list all the possible places in the PRO where a search might be profitable. Before embarking upon such a search, you should look through the many published lists of officials and the published indexes and calendars, such as that for the Patent Rolls if the office holder in question had a patent of appointment.

The Royal Archives at Windsor have a comprehensive card index of Household officials and servants. Postal enquiries are welcome.

For civil servants appointed after 1855, you should write to the Cabinet Office at the address given in Section VII.

Bibliography

Books

G E Aylmer, *The King's Servants, 1625-1642* (London, 1961)
G E Aylmer *The State's Servants, 1649-1660* (London, 1973)
Guide to the Contents of the Public Record Office (London, 1963, 1968)

Published Finding Aids

An Account of the Commissioners of Customs (1642-1909), Excise (1643-1848), Excise and Hearthmoney (1684-1689), Inland Revenue (1849-1909), and Customs and Excise (1909-1913) (London, 1913)

Calendar of Patent Rolls, Henry III to Elizabeth I (London, 1901–1982)
Calendar of State Papers, Colonial, 1513–1738 (London, 1860–1970)
Calendar of State Papers, Domestic 1547–1704 (London, 1856–1972)
Calendar of Treasury Books and Papers, 1557–1745 (London, 1868–1962)
Chronological List of Lord High Treasurers and Chief Commissioners of the Treasury, from temp. Henry VII, Appendix to the *25th Report of the Deputy Keeper of the Public Records* (London, 1864)
Colonial Office List (London, annually from 1862)
Court and City Register (London, 1742–1808)
Diplomatic Service List (London, annually from 1966)
Foreign Office List (London, annually from 1852)
Her Majesty's Letters Patent appointing Commissioners for managing, etc. the Revenue of Customs, 1671–1895 (London, 1897)
The British Imperial Calendar (London, 1810–1972, superseded by the *Civil Service Year Book)*
Lists of Sheriffs for England and Wales from the Earliest Times to A.D. 1831, PRO Lists and Indexes, vol. IX (1898)
The Royal Kalendar (London, 1767–1850)
J C Sainty (vols. I–VI), and J M Collinge (vols. VII–VIII), *Office Holders in Modern Britain,* vol. I, *Treasury Officials, 1660–1870,* vol. II, *Officials of the Secretaries of State, 1660–1782,* vol. III, *Officials of the Board of Trade, 1660–1870,* vol. IV, *Admiralty Officials, 1660–1870,* vol. V, *Home Office Officials, 1782–1870,* vol. VI, *Colonial Office Officials, 1794–1870,* vol. VII, *Navy Board Officials, 1660–1832,* vol. VIII, *Foreign Office Officials, 1782–1870* (London, 1972–1979)

Unpublished Finding Aids

Exchequer Officials, Edward I to George III MS
Justices of the Peace, 1642–1700 MS

Records (selection)

Admiralty
ADM 6   Admiralty and Secretariat Various Registers, Returns and Certificates, 1673–1960 (includes registers of baptisms, marriages and burials in dockyard and Royal Marine Churches on the Isle of Sheppey 1688–1960, and Bermuda 1826–1946).

Chancery
C213   Association Oath Rolls, 8 William III

Board of Customs and Excise
CUST 39   Establishment: Staff Lists, 1671–1922
CUST 47   Excise Board and Secretariat, Minute Books, 1695–1865
CUST 48   Excise Board and Secretariat, Entry Books of Correspondence, 1668–1839
CUST 110   Board of Excise: Irish Board and Establishment Papers, 1824–1833
CUST 116   Entry Papers of Excisemen, 1820–1870

Foreign Office
FO 366/276   Chief Clerk's Department: appointments (of King's Messengers, including baptismal certificates), 1824–1850

Lord Chamberlain's Department
LC 3   Registers of the Royal Household, 1641–1902

Lord Steward's Department
LS 13   Miscellaneous Books, 1598–1870 (see LS 13/195)

Paymaster General's Office
PMG 50   Probate Registers, 1836–1915

Public Record Office
PRO 30/19   Chapels Royal Register, 1755–1880

General Register Office
RG 4/4574   Registers of Dutch Chapel Royal, St James Palace, 1700–1754
RG 8/76–78   Whitehall Chapel Royal, marriage licences, 1687–1754
RG 8/110   Register of St James's and Windsor Chapels Royal, 1647, 1675–1709

8 Welshmen

The high incidence of common surnames and the use of patronymics make Welsh genealogy difficult. You may be able to obtain help from the Honourable Society of Cymmrodorion, and for births, marriages and deaths from 1837 you can go to St Catherine's House (see III/1 above). The National Library of Wales holds many parish registers and transcripts as well as wills, tithe records and personal and estate papers.

The three chief groups of records relevant to Welsh genealogy in the PRO are the census returns (see III/2 above), Non-parochial Registers (III/1) and wills (III/3).

Bibliography

F Jones, 'An Approach to Welsh Genealogy' *Transactions of the Honorable Society of Cymmrodorion,* Session 1948, pp. 303–466 (1949)
Guide to Genealogical Sources at the National Library of Wales, National Library of Wales leaflet

9 Irishmen

So many Irish records have been lost or destroyed that it is well worth making a preliminary approach to the Irish Genealogical Research Society for help.

The registration of births, marriages and deaths started on 1 January 1864. The records for the whole of Ireland until 1921, for Eire to date, and of non Roman Catholic marriages from 1 April 1845 are in the custody of the Registrar General in Dublin. Surviving Church of Ireland parish registers are still with the incumbents concerned or in the Irish Record Office. Roman Catholic registers seldom pre-date 1820. Unfortunately, the survival of Irish census returns is slight. Returns for 1901 and 1911 are fairly complete; D S

Begby's book lists what other returns are extant county by county (pp 63–74). Census returns are held in the Public Record Office in Dublin. Most Irish wills were destroyed by fire, although seventy two volumes of will books are preserved in the Irish Record Office. For records of land holding you should try the Registry of Deeds in Dublin. General genealogical enquiries may be made to the Genealogical Office.

The records of births, marriages and deaths in Northern Ireland since 1 January 1922 are with the Registrar General in Belfast. Many Presbyterian registers are still with the congregation, while others are held by the Presbyterian Historical Society in Belfast. This society specialises in the history of Presbyterianism and its ministers. The Public Record Office of Northern Ireland has copies and extracts of many Ulster wills, and for a fee, the Ulster Historical Foundation, at the same address, will undertake genealogical searches.

There are some records in the PRO which may be useful. These include the wills of Irishmen who died with goods in England (see III/3 above), the records of the Irish Tontines of 1773, 1775 and 1777, which cover the years 1773–1871 (see III/9 above) and the Civil List establishment for Ireland, 1709–1715 (E 403). Record relating to Irishmen in the Army are plentiful (see IV/1). There were a great number of Irishmen in the Navy (see IV/2).

Bibliography

Books

R ffolliott, *Simple Guide to Irish Genealogy* (London, 1966)
D S Begley (ed), *Irish Genealogy; a Record Finder* (Heraldic Artists, Dublin, 1982)

Published Finding Aids

Index to the Prerogative Wills of Ireland, 1536–1810, ed. Sir A Vicars

Records

Exchequer
E 403   Enrolments and Registers of Issues, Henry III to 1834 (see E 403/ 2387, Civil List Establishment, Ireland, 1709–1715)

National Debt Office
NDO 3   Irish Tontines, 1773–1871

10 Scotsmen

Civil registration started in Scotland on 1 January 1855. The records, along with many parish registers (c. 1700–1855) and census returns for 1841–1891 (every ten years), are held by the Registrar General in Edinburgh. You will find wills, judicial records, deeds, etc. in the Scottish Record Office. If you want help, you should get in touch with either the Scottish Genealogy Society, the Scots Ancestry Research Society or the Association of Scottish

Genealogists and Record Agents and for information about clans try the Scottish Tartan Society.

The PRO has the wills of Scotsmen possessed of property in the form of goods, money and investments in England (see III/3 above), and also the records of Scottish churches in England (see III/1 above and RG 4). Scotsmen are included in the Apprenticeship Books (see III/5 above) and the records of the Merchant Navy (see IV/6 above).

Bibliography

Books

G H Edwards, *In Search of Scottish Ancestry* (London, 1966)

Publishing Finding Aids

National Index of Parish Registers, vol. 2, *Sources for Scottish Genealogy and Family History,* ed. D J Steel (London, 1970)
M Stuart, *Scottish Famiy Histories held in Scottish Libraries* (Edinburgh, 1960)

Records

General Register Office
RG 4   Registers, Authenticated, 1567–1858

11 Manxmen (Isle of Man)

The registration of marriages on the Isle of Man started in 1849, and of births and deaths in 1878. The records are held by the island's General Registry, and searches of them will be made by that office for a fee. You can also obtain information about wills from the Registry, but all other records are kept in the Manx Museum Library.

The only separate records in the PRO are lists of charitable Manx bequests (HO 99).

Records

Home Office
HO 99   Channel Islands etc., Entry Books, 1760–1921 (see HO 99/22)

12 Channel Islanders

Jersey

The records of births, marriages and deaths in Jersey commenced in 1842. Registers of births, non-Anglican marriages and deaths are held by the Registrars of the Island's twelve parishes while the registers of marriages in the Anglican Church are held by the rectors and vicars. Duplicate registers of all births, marriages and deaths are held by the Superintendent Registrar and he, like the Parochial Registrars and the clergy, can undertake searches and issue certified extracts from those registers in his custody. The Superintendent Registrar is unable to undertake genealogical research of a general nature. In such cases the enquirer is advised to contact either the Société Jersiaise or The Channel Islands Family History Society, one of whose members may be prepared to assist in the research. Records of baptism, marriage and burial prior to 1842 do exist and these are held by the rectors and vicars who are able to issue extracts from the registers in their custody.

Guernsey, Alderney and Sark

Civil registration of births, deaths and non-Anglican marriages in Guernsey began in 1840; in Alderney in 1850; and in Sark, deaths in 1915, marriages in 1919 and births in 1925. From 1919 all marriages and from 1925 all births and deaths in Guernsey, Alderney and Sark have been registered centrally in Guernsey by Her Majesty's Greffier in his capacity as Registrar-General of Births, Deaths and Marriages. Enquiries relating to Alderney should be addressed to the Clerk of the Court; and to Sark to Mr Hilary Carré, Registrar.

Deeds, judicial records and wills may be consulted by searchers in person at the Greffe; all are indexed. Permission to consult wills of personalty from 1664 should be obtained from the Registrar of the Ecclesiastical Court. Microfilm copies of the 1841–1881 census returns for Guernsey, Alderney and Sark are also held at the Greffe.

Files on leading Island families are held at the Priaulx Library, St Peter Port.

Pre-civil registration records are held by the rectors of the ten Guernsey parishes and the vicars of Alderney and Sark.

Bibliography

Books

L R Burnes, 'Genealogical Research in the Channel Isles' *Genealogists' Magazine*, vol. XIX, pp. 169–172
J Conway Davies, 'The Records of the Royal Courts', La Société Guernesiaise, *Transactions* XVI (1956–60) pp. 404–14
David W Le Poidevin, 'How to Trace your Ancestors in Guernsey' (Taunton, 1978)

Published Finding Aids

List of Records in the Greffe, Guernsey
Volume 1 (List and Index Society, 1969)
Volume 2 (List and Index Society, 1978)
Additional lists may be consulted in typescript at the Greffe

13 Protestant Nonconformists

Any extant nonconformist registers (of baptisms, burials and some marriages) are either in the PRO, with the congregation, or deposited locally (see III/1, above). If you are looking for Independent/Congregational clergy, the index at Dr Williams' Library should be helpful, and you will find there, in addition, an excellent collection of other material relating to nonconformist history in general.

For help on specific noncomformist sects, you would be well advised to write to the relevant central office. The Quakers (Society of Friends), for example, have a library in London with particularly comprehensive and well kept records, of which many are in print. They also have the indexes to the Quaker registers in the PRO (RG 6). The PRO has rolls of Quaker attorneys for the period 1831–1835 (E 3) and 1836–1842 (CP 10). Indexes to the Exchequer rolls are found by reference to the Catalogue of Lists and Indexes, Exchequer.

The Baptists and the United Reformed Church (Presbyterians and Congregationalists) both have historical societies, and the John Rylands Library in Manchester has records relating to the Unitarians and Presbyterians. The records of the central registry of London Independents, Presbyterians and Baptists, 1742–1837, are in the PRO (Dr Williams' collection, RG 4, original certificates in RG 5. The latter are particularly useful as they give the name of the child's maternal grandfather.). The Methodists (Wesleyans) have their own archival collection in Manchester. The registers of the Wesleyan Metropolitan Registry at Paternoster Row (baptisms in England and Wales, 1808–1888) are in the PRO (RG 4). You should bear in mind that the early followers of Wesley will appear in the parish registers of the established Church.

The PRO has the enrolments of nonconformist trust deeds from 1736 (C 54).

Bibliography

Books

N Graham, *The Genealogists' Consolidated Guide to Nonconformist and Foreign Registers in Inner London, 1538–1837* (Birchington, 1980)
Rev. William Leary, ed. Michael Gandy, *My Ancestor was a Methodist* (Soc. Gen., 1982)
H G Tibbutt, 'Sources for Congregational Church Records', *Transactions of the Congregational History Society*, XIX (1960–1964), pp. 147–155, 230–236
E Welsh, 'The Early Methodists and their Records', *Journal of the Society of Archivists*, IV (1971), p. 210
D J Steel, *Sources of Nonconformist Genealogy and Family History* (London 1973)
Non Conformist Congregations in Britain (Dr. Williams's Trust, London, 1973)

Unpublished Finding Aids

Catalogue of Lists and Indexes, Exchequer, TS

Records

Chancery
C 54 Close Rolls

Common Pleas
CP 10 Oath Rolls, 1779–1847

Exchequer
E 3 Attorneys' Oath Rolls, 1830–1875

General Register Office
RG 4 Registers, Authenticated, 1567–1858, including Dr Williams' Registry
(RG 4/4658–4676); Paternoster Row Registry (RG 4/4680 (index),
4677–4679).
RG 5 Non-parochial certificates, 1742–1840
RG 6 Registers, Authenticated, Society of Friends, 1613–1841

14 Roman Catholics

The registers of Catholic churches are either in PRO the (see III/1 above) or
with the congregation. If you need help in tracing Catholic ancestors, you
should try the relevant diocesan archivist or the Catholic Central Library. A
recently formed society, the English Catholic Ancestor, aims at the acquiring
and disseminating of information about Catholic families. The Catholic
Record Society has published a great deal of useful material. Burials of
Catholics often took place in the parish churchyard and the records are,
therefore, in the parish registers.

Records of Catholics in the PRO are largely the records of their persecution,
and their bulk accordingly varies with fluctuations in anti-popery. The
Recusant Rolls (E 376 and E 377) are annual returns of dissenters (Protestant
and Catholic) who had their property forfeit or were fined, 1592–1691. They
are the major offenders. You will find a lot on the persecutions in county
record offices. Most Catholics supported the King in the Civil War, so their
estates may be referred to in *Calendars of the Committee for Compounding with
Delinquents.* There are many inventories of Catholic possessions in the State
Papers for the Interregnum (SP 28). From the reign of George I and the
Jacobite risings, there are lists of papists who forfeited their estates (E 174,
KB 18, FEC 1). From this period Catholic wills were enrolled in the
Recovery Rolls of the Court of Common Pleas (CP 43). There are lists of
Catholic attorneys for the period 1830–1875 (E 3) and 1790–1836 (CP 10).
Indexes to the former may be found in the Catalogue of Lists and Indexes,
Exchequer.

Bibliography

Books

Bibliographical Studies, vols. I–III, changed to *Recusant History,* from vol. IV, the
Journal of the Catholic Record Society (Bognor Regis, 1951 to date)

Catholic Directory (London, annually from 1837)
Catholic Record Society, publications (1905–1980)
D J Steel and E R Samuel, *Sources for Roman Catholic and Jewish Genealogy and Family History, National Index of Parish Registers vol. 3* (London, 1974)

Unpublished Finding Aids

Catalogue of Lists and Indexes, CP and KB, TS
Catalogue of Lists and Indexes, Exchequer, TS

Published Finding Aids

Calendar of State Papers, Domestic, Committee for Compounding with Delinquents, 1643–1660 (London, 1889–1893)
Sources for the History of Roman Catholics in England, ed. J H Pollen, SPCK Helps for Students of History, no. 39

Records

Court of Common Pleas
CP 10   Attorneys; Oath Rolls, 1790–1836
CP 43   Recovery Rolls, 25 Elizabeth I to 1837 (indexes in IND 16943–9, 17183–17216)

Exchequer
E 3   Exchequer of Pleas, Attorneys' Oath Rolls, 1830–1972
E 174   Returns of Papists' Estates, George I
E 376   Pipe Office, Recusant Rolls, Chancellor Series, 34 Elizabeth I to 1 and 2 William and Mary
E 377   Pipe Office, Recusant Rolls, Clerk of the Pipe, 34 Elizabeth I to 1 and 2 William and Mary

Forfeited Estates Commission
FEC 1   Papers, 1552–1744 (Returns of Papists' estates following the 1715 rebellion cf. E 174)

Court of King's Bench
KB 18   Returns of Papists in Lancaster, George I

State Paper Office
SP 28   Commonwealth Exchequer Papers, 1642–1660 (see SP 28/217A and B)

15 Foreigners in Britain

The records of naturalisations and denizations are kept in the PRO (HO 1-HO 3, HO 5), but the majority of aliens settling in Britain did not go through the legal formalities and so do not appear. Indexes have been published for the period 1603–1935.

For immigrants between 1878 and 1960, arriving from places outside Europe by sea, the Passenger Lists are an additional source of information (BT 26). You will find name, age, occupation and address in the United Kingdom, and date of entry into the country but no indication of the intended length of stay. After 1906 the Registers of Passenger Lists (BT 32) give, under the different ports, the names of the ships and the date of arrival. The Passenger Lists have not been preserved after 1960, and there are none for arrivals by air.

The registers of some 'foreign' churches in England, in particular refugee churches (RG 4), and the church of the Russian Orthodox community in London (RG 8), are in the PRO. Another source is the records of annuities and pensions paid to refugees for services to the Crown among the Treasury Papers and Paymaster General's Papers. These include, for instance, allowances to Polish refugees, 1828–1856, Spaniards, 1855–1909, Frenchmen 1793–1831, American loyalist pensions, 1780–1855 and accounts concerning refugees from Corsica, Malta, Holland and Santo Domingo (PMG 53, T 1, T 50, T 93). An important group of refugees was that of the exiles from the Palatinate, shipped from Holland to England in 1709, many of whom remained in England rather than continuing to the New World. There are embarkation lists, received by the British resident in the Hague, of those leaving Holland, now among the Treasury files (T 1). There are references to them also in the State papers (SP 84) and the Colonial Office records (CO 388), and you can find many wills of bi-national Dutchmen in the records of the PCC (see III/3 above). For records of Poles in the British armed forces in Second World War see page 37.

You will find a large number of early references to aliens resident in England in the Chancery and Exchequer records, concerning, for example, alien clergy, foreign merchants, and alien priories (C 47, C 54, C 65, C 66, E 106).

If you have any enquiries about recent naturalisation, you should write to the Home Office.

a Huguenots
Huguenots were French protestants fleeing from religious persecution from the 1550s onwards, and in large numbers after the Revocation of the Edict of Nantes (which had granted toleration to them) in 1685. It is quite possible, however, for a Huguenot ancestor to appear in this country some time after this, as many fled first to Holland or Germany and only later moved to England. If you think this might be the case, you should get in touch with the Huguenot Society of Germany, or the Central Bureau of Genealogy of Holland. There are often strong family traditions of Huguenot descent, and names are usually a good indication of such a background.

The main Huguenot settlements were in London, Norwich, Canterbury, Southampton, Rye, Sandwich, Colchester, Bristol, Plymouth, Thorney and various places in Ireland. There are no known records of any communities which may have existed in the Midlands or the North of England, and there is little on settlement in Scotland. It is, naturally, more difficult to trace a family which struck out on its own to a new part of the country, where no French church existed and they used the local parish church for baptisms. Huguenot burial records are rare at all times, and by the nineteenth century almost non-existent, except for the records of deaths of the inmates of the London Huguenot Hospital, which are in the Huguenot Library.

A great deal has been published by the Huguenot Society of London, and you should start by looking at that readily available material. There is a Huguenot Library in London, which you can use by arrangement with the Honorary Librarian. No personal callers can be seen but the staff will undertake a brief search for you, for a fee. You will also find Huguenot material in other areas where they settled, in the Cathedral Library at Canterbury, the County Record Office at Norwich and the City Record Office at Southampton, for instance.

Most of the sources for Huguenot genealogy in the PRO have been included in Huguenot Society publications in some form. The published *Calendars of State Papers* are also useful as are the various lists in print, of aliens resident in England, naturalised, or taking oaths of allegiance (compiled from the record classes E 169, E 179, E 196, KB 24, RG 4, SP 10–SP 12, SP 44).

b French Emigrés
A French sounding name can also be the result of descent from refugees from the Revolution. There are many letters and papers concerning such people among Home Office (HO 69), Privy Council (PC 1), Foreign Office (FO 95) and War Office papers (WO 1), from 1789 to 1814. In addition, the Treasury had a French Refugees Relief Committee, 1792–1828 (T 50, T 93), the records of which give names of people receiving pensions.

c Jews
There were Jews in England in the early Middle Ages but descent from members of this early community is virtually impossible to trace. There has been regular Jewish immigration since the seventeenth century, and a steady rate of assimilation into the gentile population, so you may well find a Jewish element in your ancestry. The immigrants were of two sorts: Sephardim (Portuguese, Spanish and Italian), arriving from 1657 onwards; and Ashkenazim (German and East European). The first of the Ashkenazim came in the 1680s from Holland and Bohemia, but the main influx was of Russians and Poles in the last three decades of the nineteenth century, many of whom were in the clothing trade. You can usually tell which sort of Jew your ancestor was from his name.

The registers of the London Sephardic Synagogue (established in 1701) are in Portuguese, and are partly published. The registers of the Ashkenazim are in Yiddish before 1840, and are not very easily accessible as they are mostly held by the congregations concerned. Many of them, however, are included in the Mormon International Genealogical Index (see III/1 above), and this many well be the best place to start, having traced the family as far as possible through the registers of births, marriages and deaths at St Catherine's House (III/1 above). You can find the names and addresses of synagogues in the Jewish Year Book, and for help on London Ashkenazi Jewry from Rev. J. Sunshine in the Offices of the United Synagogue. There are records there of the three old London synagogues from 1709, and they will search these for a fee. You should write for help on the London Sephardic community to the Honorary Genealogist at the Spanish and Portuguese Synagogue where the records are kept. The Anglo Jewish Archives in the Mocatta Library have an invaluable collection of Jewish pedigrees compiled by Sir Thomas Colyer Fergusson and many other Jewish sources.

The most productive sources for specifically Jewish genealogy at the PRO are wills, naturalisation papers and records of change of name. There is a sizeable collection of pre-1858 Jewish wills (about 5% of the Jewish population made wills, and all of them were proved in the PCC; see III/3 above), and they can be most informative as Jewish assets were often in the form of cash and chattels because they were banned from legal landownership. For naturalisation see above in this section, and for change of name, which was quite usual for Jewish immigrants because of persecution see III/4 above.

Bibliography

Books

My Ancestor was Jewish, ed. M Gandy (Society of Genealogists, 1982)
Anglo-Jewish Bibliography, 1937-1970, ed. R P Lehmann (London, 1973)
Anglo-Jewish Notabilities, their Arms and Testamentary Dispositions (Jewish Historical Society of England, London, 1949)
Magna Bibliotheca Anglo-Judaica, ed. C Roth (London, 1937)
J M Ross, 'Naturalisation of Jews in Britain', *Transactions of the Jewish Historical Society of England,* vol. 24 (1975), pp. 59–72
W S Samuel, 'Sources of Anglo-Jewish Genealogy', *Genealogists' Magazine,* vol. VI (1932), pp. 146–159
E R Samuel, 'Jewish Ancestors and where to find them', *Genealogists' Magazine,* vol. XI (1953), pp. 414–441

Published Finding Aids

Bevis Marks Records, Registers of the London Sephardic Synagogue (Oxford, 1940–1949)
Calendar of Close Rolls, 1227-1509 (London, 1892–1963)
Calendar of Patent Rolls, 1216-1578 (London, 1894–1982)
Calendar of State Papers, Domestic Series, 1547-1704 (London, 1856–1972)
Calendar of Treasury Papers, 1557-1728 (London 1868–1889)
H S Q Henriques, *The Jews and the English Law* (London, 1908)
Home Office Certificates of Naturalisation, Index, 1844-1935 (London, 1908–1937)
The Jewish Yearbook (London, annually from 1896)
R E G Kirk, *Returns of Aliens in London, 1523-1603* (Huguenot Society, Vol. X, London, 1900–1908)
W A Knittle, *Early Eighteenth Century Palatine Emigration* (Philadelphia, 1937)
List of Jewish persons endenizenised and naturalised, 1609-1799, ed. R D Barnett and A J Diamond (Jewish Historical Society of England, London, 1970)

L D MacWethy, *The Book of Names especially relating to the early Palatines and the First Settlers in the Mohawk Valley* (New York, 1933)

National Index of Parish Registers, vol. III, *Sources for Roman Catholic and Jewish Genealogy and Family History,* ed. D Steel and E R Samuel (London 1974)

New York Genealogical and Biographical Records, vols. XL and XLI (New York, 1909 1910)

W Page, *Denization and Naturalisation of Aliens in England 1509–1603* (Huguenot Society Publications, vol. VIII, Lymington, 1893)

Registers of Churches, of Huguenots in London and elsewhere, (Huguenot Society, London, 1887–1956)

C Roth, *Archives of the United Synagogue, Report and Catalogue* (London, 1930)

Rotuli Parliamentorum, Edward I to Henry VII (London, 1783, Index, London, 1832)

W A Shaw, *Letters of Denization and Acts of Naturalisation for Aliens in England, 1603–1800* (Huguenot Society, Lymington, 1911, Manchester, 1923 and London, 1932)

Unpublished Finding Aids

Immigrants: Documents in the Public Record Office, PRO leaflet no. 6

Index to Denizations, 1801–1873, and to Acts of Naturalisation, 1801–1935, TS

Indexes of 'Foreign' Churches, MS

Index of Memorials for Denizations and Naturalisations, 1835–1844, MS

B Lloyd, List and Registers of Dutch Chapel Royal, 1689–1825, TS

Records

Board of Trade
BT 26   Passenger Lists, Inwards, 1878–1960
BT 32   Registers of Passenger Lists, 1906–1951

Chancery
C 47   Miscellanea, Bundle 13, foreign merchants, Henry III to Henry VIII; 15–21, alien clergy, John to William and Mary
C 54   Close Rolls, 6 John to 1903 (containing enrolments of naturalisation certificates, 1844–1873)
C 65   Parliament Rolls, 1 Edward III to 3 and 4 Elizabeth II
C 66   Patent Rolls, 3 John to 9 George VI

Colonial Office
CO 388   Board of Trade, Original Correspondence, 1654–1792

Exchequer
E 106   Extents of Alien Priories, etc. 22 Edward I to 22 Edward IV
E 169   Oaths of Allegiance, etc., 1709–1868
E 179   Subsidy Rolls, Henry VIII to William and Mary (for lists of foreigners in London, 1423–1581)
E 196   Sacrament Certificates, 1700–1827

Foreign Office
FO 95   Miscellanea, 1639–1942

Home Office
HO 1   Denizations and Naturalisations, 1789–1871 (index in HO 5/25–32)
HO 2   Certificates of Aliens, 1836–1852
HO 3   Returns and Papers, 1836–1869
HO 5   Aliens Entry Books, 1794–1921 (index to HO 2, HO 5/25–32)
HO 45   Registered Papers, 1839–1950 (denizations and naturalisations, 1841–1878, see HO 144)
HO 69   Bouillon Papers, 1789–1809
HO 144 Registered Papers, Supplementary, 1878–1947 (closed for up to 100 years)

Court of King's Bench
KB 24   Swearing or Oath Rolls, 1673–1906 (published in Huguenot Society, vol. XXVII)

Privy Council Office
PC 1   Papers, 1481–1946

Paymaster General's Office
PMG 53 Allowances to Polish Refugees and Distressed Spaniards, 1855–1909

General Register Office
RG 4   Registers, Authenticated, 1567–1858
RG 8   Registers, Unauthenticated, Miscellaneous, 1646–1970

State Paper Office
SP 10   State Papers, Domestic, Edward VI
SP 11   State Papers, Domestic, Mary I
SP 12   State Papers, Domestic, Elizabeth I
SP 44   Entry Books, 1661–1828 (for denizations, 1681–1688 see SP 44/67)
SP 84   State Papers, Foreign, Holland, 1585–1780

Treasury
T 1   Treasury Board Papers, 1557–1920 (for pensions to refugees)
T 50   Documents relating to Refugees, 1780–1856
T 93   French Refugees' Relief Committee, 1792–1828

War Office
WO 1   In-Letters, 1732–1868

16 British Nationals Abroad

The records of colonial registration of births, marriages and deaths are usually still in the country concerned.

If you are looking for information concerning someone who served abroad in the Colonial or Foreign Services, you should look among the relevant records in the PRO (CO, DO, FO). The records of the Levant Company are among the State Papers (SP), and those of companies trading to Africa are among the Treasury records (T). For British nationals abroad, but not necessarily in an official capacity there are various registers of births, marriages and deaths which may be helpful. Some of these from British embassies and consulates are among the Foreign Office records (FO), but most of them were held by the Registrar General (RG 32–RG 36, RG 43). Most of the foreign registers date from the 1830s with the exception of Paris (from 1784), the Hague (from 1627), Rotterdam (from 1708) and Leghorn (from 1707). There are also registers of births, marriages and deaths at sea (BT 158–BT 160), and some death certificates for France and Belgium for 1914–1921 (RG 35).

The General Register Office has army chaplains' returns (1796–1880), regimental returns (1761–1924), army registers (1881–1959), service department registers from 1 April 1959 and War Deaths (1914–1920 and 1939–1948). As well as these registers, the General Register Office has an index of the Foreign Registers at the PRO. Many records of baptisms, marriages and burials abroad for the years 1706–1939, mainly from Anglican congregations, are preserved in the Guildhall and Lambeth Palace Libraries. A topographical guide to the location of all the known records of foreign registrations will be published shortly by the Guildhall Library.

Births, deaths and marriages at sea were recorded in the ship's log and can only be found (pre-1837) if the ship's name is known. From 1837 the records are at the General Register Office in St Catherine's House. From 1854 these are in the registers in the PRO. The tradition associating baptisms at sea with St Dunstan's, Stepney, is fallacious (see article by A D Ridge).

The wills of Britons who died abroad were proved in the Prerogative Court of Canterbury if they left any assets in Britain, and are thus now in the PRO (see III/3 above).

Bibliography

Abstract of Arrangements respecting Registration of Births, Marriages and Deaths, etc. (London, 1952)

I A Baxter, *Brief Guide to Biographical Sources in the India Office Library* (London, 1979)

Guildhall Library, Parish Registers, a Handlist, Part III (1967) (for registers of Anglican congregations abroad)

The Records of the Colonial and Dominions Offices, PRO Handbook No. 3, (London, 1964)

The Records of the Foreign Office, 1782–1939, PRO Handbook No 13 (London, 1969)

A D Ridge, 'All at Sea', *Archives,* VI (1964) pp. 229–234

Unpublished Finding Aids

List of birth, marriage and death registers in Foreign Office Embassy and Consular records, TS.

Records

Board of Trade
BT 158   Registers and Indexes of Births, Marriages and Deaths of Passengers at Sea, 1854–1890

BT 159   Registers of Deaths at Sea of British Nationals, 1875–1888
BT 160   Registers of Births at Sea of British Nationals, 1875–1891

CO   Colonial Office records

DO   Dominions Office records

FO   Foreign Office records

General Register Office
RG 32   Miscellaneous Foreign Returns, 1831–1946 (index in RG 43)
RG 33   Foreign Registers and Returns, 1627–1958 (index in RG 43)
RG 34   Foreign Marriages, 1826–1921 (index in RG 43)
RG 35   Foreign Deaths, 1830–1921 (index in RG 43)
RG 36   Registers and Returns of Births, Marriages and Deaths in the
        Protectorates, etc. of Africa and Asia, 1895–1945 (index in RG 43)
RG 43   Miscellaneous Foreign Returns of Births, Marriages and Deaths,
        Indexes, 1627–1947 (index to RG 32–RG 36)

State Paper Office
SP 110/70 Register of births, marriages and deaths, Aleppo, 1756–1800
        (Levant Company)

Treasury
T 70   African Companies, 1660–1833

17 Emigrants

The PRO has many records relating to emigration but, because of the nature
and limited scope of many of them, there can be no certainty of finding
information on any particular individual.

Passenger Lists are very rare from before 1800, and there was no regular
series of them kept until 1890. Thereafter, you will find them arranged by
year under the names of the ports of departure, and they give name, age,
occupation and some sort of address of the passenger (BT 27). There are
Registers of Passenger Lists (BT 32) which are helpful in indicating the ships
leaving each port. Prior to 1920 only the month, not the exact date, of
departure is given.

It was not common, before the First World War, for passports to be issued to
people travelling abroad. A few were, in particular the Exchequer Licences to
Pass Beyond the Seas (E 157) which include lists and registers of soldiers
taking the Oath of Allegiance before going to serve in the Low Countries
(1613–1624); people going abroad, mainly to Holland (1624–1632); and
passengers bound for New England, Barbados, Maryland, Virginia and other
colonies (1634–1639 and 1677).* For the period 1795–1948 the Foreign Office
Passport Registers (FO 610, FO 611) have entries of names and intended
destinations abroad of all applicants for passports, but before 1915 these were

---

* All indexed by J C Hotten (see bibliography).

almost all for official Foreign Office travel or for people going on the Grand Tour of Europe.

The Treasury (T) handled a considerable volume of colonial business, and you may find useful references in the published calendars, which will lead you to the original books and papers. The Privy Council was also involved, receiving, for example, petitions from colonists, warrants for grants or surrenders of office, instructions to governors and warrants for letters of marque (PC 1, PC 2, PC 5).

Many emigrants had assistance with their passage from the parish under the provisions of the 1834 Poor Law. The records, which are normally lists of emigrants giving occupations and destinations, are arranged by counties and Poor Law Unions, so you will need to know where the emigrant came from (MH 12).

The correspondence of the Colonial Office (CO) contains a class of letters (CO 384) concerning emigration, including letters from settlers or from people hoping to settle in the colonies between 1817 and 1896. You may also find, among other correspondence files, details of land grants and applications for them, although you may have a long search.

There are one or two more places where a very long search, with inadequate finding aids, may be successful. The Admiralty records include, for instance, medical journals from emigrant ships and convict ships (ADM 101); and registers of convicts (ADM 6) and troops (ADM 108, MT 23) shipped to various parts of the world. The Audit Office accounts have references to pensions paid to colonists (AO 1-AO 3), and the Chancery Patent Rolls (C 66) contain entries relating to grants of offices and lands in America and elsewhere.

a North Americans
Owing to the fact that there was no regular series of passenger lists or passports until relatively recently, that there was no central registrations of births, marriages and deaths before 1837 (1855 in Scotland), and that there is no national index of parish registers, you are very unlikely to identify an individual, unless you know the place of origin, if the family emigrated before 1837 (or 1855 from Scotland). The International Genealogical Index of baptisms (see III/1 above) may be a good place to start if you need to find the place of origin, but your success will depend largely on how common the surname is. It is essential that you should do some preliminary work from published means of reference, and if possible, among records in the U.S.A. or Canada to try to establish at least the port and date of entry.

Among the registers of the Treasury are four volumes (T 47/9-12) which give details of emigrants going from England, Wales and Scotland to the New World between 1773 and 1776. The information in those for England and Wales has been summarised in the card index, which gives name, age, occupation, reason for leaving the country, last place of residence, date of departure, and destination. Deportees for the period 1615–1775 have been listed in P W Coldham's *Bonded Passengers to America*. For the period 1719–1744, the Treasury records also contain Money Warrants (T 53) which include lists of felons transported to the American colonies.

Some information on colonists can be found in the correspondence and papers of the Colonial Office (CO), which cover the West Indies as well as the continent of America, and start in 1574. More detail on tracts of land in West and East New Jersey, Pennsylvania, New England and elsewhere is in the records of the West New Jersey Society (TS 12), a company formed in 1691 for the division of the land. There are many names in the correspondence, minute books, share transfers, deeds and claims. There are records relating to slave owners in the West Indies, 1812–1846 among Treasury, Audit Office and National Debt Office papers (T 71, AO 14, NDO 4).

During and after the American War of Independence, many people suffered losses on account of their loyalty to the British Crown, and were entitled to claim compensation under the Treaty of Peace in 1783 and a new Treaty of Amity between Great Britain and the United States of America in 1794. The Treasury records contain the reports of commissioners investigating individual claims, and some compensation and pension lists, 1780–1835 (T 50, T 79). Commissioners were also appointed in 1802, and their papers contain lists of claimants of pensions, and papers supporting their claims (AO 12, AO 13). The Declared Accounts of the Audit Office (AO 1) contain the accounts of payments and pensions made. Similar claims for compensation to loyalists were made when East Florida was ceded to Spain in 1783, and they are now among the Treasury records (T 77).

Americans who died with goods in the United Kingdom had their wills proved in the Prerogative Court of Canterbury, so they are now to be found among the PCC records in the PRO (see III/3 above). They have been indexed by P W Coldham (1600–1858).

The Genealogical Society of Utah has a huge index containing a great deal of information from British sources, including microfilm copies of the 1841–1881 Census Returns; and photocopies, microfilms and transcripts of much of the PRO's American material can be consulted in the Library of Congress, some state libraries, and the Public Archives of Canada. You can obtain copies of PRO publications from the British Information Services. There are several genealogical societies that may be worth contacting, in particular the National Genealogical Society in Washington, and the Ontario, British Columbia, Saskatchewan and Alberta Societies.

b Australians and New Zealanders
Until the Passenger Lists begin in 1890 (BT 27) there are few records relating to voluntary emigrants; you will find far more extensive documentation of condemned deportees. The fact that a man's family also travelled to the colony does not mean that he was not a convict, as many 'came free' rather than remain in England.

The principal source for convicts is the series of Transportation Registers (HO 11) which contain lists of convicts carried in the transport ships; each volume has an index of ships' names. In the lists you will find the full names of each convict, the term of his or her transportation, and the date and place of conviction. This last piece of information may enable you to search for further details in the Criminal Registers and the Assize Court records.

The Criminal Registers (HO 26, HO 27), which begin in 1791 for Middlesex and 1805 for all other counties in England and Wales, record the names of all people charged with indictable offences and sometimes give personal details. Assize records (ASSI) can provide details about felons who were sentenced to death on conviction for such crimes as manslaughter, horse-stealing and house-breaking, but were afterwards reprieved and sentenced to transportation. Unless, however, you already have precise information from the Registers on the date and place of conviction, a search of the records of the Assizes would be a daunting task.

A series of censuses of the convict population of New South Wales and Tasmania was made at intervals between 1788 and 1859 (HO 10), which include the names of members of convicts' families, who either 'came free' or were 'born in the colony' as well as the convicts themselves. The census of 1828 is the most complete and is now in print. It contains the names of more than 35,000 people, with their ages, religions, families, residences, occupations and details of stock and land held. In addition there is an indication of whether each person came to the colony free or in bond, or was born in the colony, and of the ship and year of arrival. Some of the earlier censuses also give details of the date and place of trial in England.

Colonial Office (CO) correspondence, entry books and registers contain material which may be of use, including lists of emigrant settlers and convicts, 1801–1821 (CO 201). There are also some useful War Office papers, relating to Army pensioners who were encouraged to emigrate to New South Wales and New Zealand (WO 1, WO 43).

Many of the records of transportation to Australia have been indexed by the Society of Australian Genealogists, who can also offer help and advice. There are microfilms of many PRO records concerning Australia at the National Library in Canberra and the Mitchell Library, Sydney. Genealogists in New Zealand should get in touch with the New Zealand Society of Genealogists.

c South Africans
There is some material in the PRO on settlers and grants of land among the correspondence, entry books and registers of the Colonial Office (CO 48, CO 49, CO 336, CO 462), beginning in 1795. The Genealogical Society of South Africa will give advice.

d The British in India
The records of the British in India, including the registration of baptisms, marriages and burials, and also wills, are preserved among the India Office Records.

e Emigrants to France

Help in tracing English families who settled in France may be obtained from the French Research Organisation for Genealogical Services.

Bibliography

Books

I A Baxter, *Brief Guide to Biographical Sources in the India Office Library* (London, 1979)

R H Ellis, 'Records of the American Loyalists' Claims in the Public Record Office', *Genealogists' Magazine,* vol. XII (1958) pp. 375–378, 407–410, 433–435.

J S W Gibson, 'Assisted Pauper Emigration, 1834–1837', *Genealogists' Magazine,* vol. XX (1982) pp. 374–375

H B Guppy, *Homes of Family Names in Great Britain* (Baltimore, 1968)

M and J Kaminkow, *Emigrants in Bondage* (Baltimore, 1967)

The Records of the Colonial and Dominions Offices, PRO Handbook No. 3 (London, 1964)

Published Finding Aids

Acts of the Privy Council of England, Colonial Series, 1613–1783 (London, 1908–1912)

Alphabetical Guide to War Office and other Military Records preserved in the Public Record Office, PRO Lists and Indexes, LIII (London, 1931)

C M Andrews, *Guide to the Materials for American History to 1793 in the Public Record Office of Great Britain* (Washington, 1912 and 1914)

C E Banks and E E Brownell, *Topographical Dictionary of 2885 English Emigrants to New England, 1620–1650* (New York, 1963, 1976)

Calendar of State Papers, Colonial, America and West Indies, 1574–1738 (London, 1860–1969)

Calendar of Treasury Books, 1660–1718 (London, 1904–1962)

Calendar of Treasury Papers, 1557–1728 (London, 1868–1889)

Calendar of Treasury Books and Papers, 1729–1745 (London, 1898–1903)

P W Coldham, *Bonded Passengers to America* (Baltimore, 1983). Lists deportees 1651–1775; compiled from Assize records, Patent Rolls, Quarter Sessions records, Treasury papers and records in the Corporation of London Record Office

P W Coldham, *English Estates of American Colonists* (Baltimore, 1980), covering 1600–1858

P W Coldham, *American Loyalist Claims,* National Genealogical Society (Washington, 1980) (index to AO 13/1–35, 37, claims from loyalists who escaped to Canada, 1774–1793)

P W Coldham, *Lord Mayor's Court of London, Depositions relating to America, 1641–1736,* National Genealogical Society (Washington, 1980)

Passenger and Immigration Lists Bibliography 1538–1900, ed. W P Filby (Michigan, 1981)

Passenger and Immigration Lists Index, ed. W P Filby and M K Meyer (Michigan, 1981) 3 volumes

Guide to Genealogical Research in the National Archives (Washington, 1982)

J C Hotten, *Original Lists of Persons emigrating to America, 1600–1700* (London, 1874)

C B Jewson, *Transcript of Three Registers of Passengers from Great Yarmouth to Holland and New England, 1637–1639*, Norfolk Record Society, vol. XXV (1954)

Journals of the Board of Trade and Plantations, 1704–1782 (London, 1920–1938)

J and M Kaminkow, *A List of Emigrants from England to America, 1718–1759* (Baltimore, 1964)

A H Lancour, *A Bibliography of Ships' Passenger Lists, 1538–1825* (New York, 1963)

List of Colonial Office Records, PRO Lists and Indexes, vol. XXXVI (London, 1911)

List of Records of the Treasury, Paymaster General's Office, Exchequer and Audit Department and Board of Trade, prior to 1837, PRO Lists and Indexes No. XLVI (London, 1922)

New South Wales: Census . . . November 1828, ed. M R Sainty and K A Johnson (Sydney, 1980)

New World Immigrants, ed. M Tepper (Baltimore, 1980) (a consolidation of passenger lists)

List of State Papers, Domestic, 1547–1792, and Home Office Records, 1782–1837, PRO Lists and Indexes, vol. XLIII (London, 1914)

L L Robson, *The Convict Settlers of Australia* (Melbourne, 1965)

Ships Passenger Lists, ed. Carl Boyer, 3 vols. *The South* (1538–1825), *National and New England* (1600–1825), *New York and New Jersey* (1600–1825) (Newhall, California, 1980)

Unpublished Finding Aids

Card index to Treasury Registers of emigrants (T 47/9–12)

Indexes to Chancery Patent Rolls, 1 Elizabeth I–22 George V, MS

Index to Colonial Office, New South Wales Original Correspondence, 1823–1833, TS (also available at the Mitchell Library, Sydney and Melbourne Public Library)

Index of Names to American Loyalist Claims (AO 12 and 13), TS

Records

Admiralty
ADM 6   Registers, Returns and Certificates, 1673–1859 (for registers of convicts on ships, 1819–1834)
ADM 101   Medical Journals (include emigrant ships 1815–1853, convict ships, 1817–1853)
ADM 108   Admiralty Transport Department Records, 1773–1837

Exchequer and Audit Office
AO 1   Declared Accounts, 1536–1828
AO 2   Declared and Passed Accounts, 1803–1848
AO 3   Accounts, Various, 1539–1886
AO 12   American Loyalists' Claims, 1776–1831

AO 13   American Loyalists' Claims, 1780–1835

AO 14   Claims, Various, 1795–1846

ASSI   Clerks of Assize

Board of Trade
BT 27   Passenger Lists, Outwards, 1890–1960
BT 32   Registers of Passenger Lists, 1906–1951

Chancery
C 66   Patent Rolls, 3 John to 9 George VI

Colonial Office
CO 1   Colonial Papers, General, 1574–1757
CO 5   America, Original Correspondence, 1606–1807
CO 48   Cape of Good Hope, Original Correspondence, 1807–1910
CO 49   Cape of Good Hope, Entry Books, 1795–1872
CO 201 New South Wales, Original Correspondence, 1784–1900
CO 202 New South Wales, Entry Books, 1786–1873
CO 207 Entry Books relating to Convicts (microfilm), 1788–1868
CO 323 Colonies, General, Original Correspondence, 1689–1940
CO 324 Colonies General, Entry Books, 1740, 1791–1872
CO 336 Cape of Good Hope, Registers, 1850–1910
CO 360 New South Wales, Registers, 1849–1900
CO 369 New South Wales, Out Letters, 1873–1900
CO 381 Colonies General, Entry Books, 1740, 1791–1872
CO 384 Emigration, Original Correspondence, 1817–1896
CO 385 Emigration, Entry Books, 1814–1871
CO 386 Land and Emigration Commission, 1833–1894
CO 391 Board of Trade, Minutes, 1675–1782
CO 462 Cape of Good Hope, Register of Out-Letters, 1872–1910

Exchequer
E 157   Licences to Pass Beyond the Seas, Elizabeth I to 1677
E 370   Lord Treasurers' Remembrancer and Pipe Office, Miscellaneous Rolls,
          Henry II to 1840

Foreign Office
FO 610 Passport Registers, 1795–1943 (index in FO 611)
FO 611 Indexes of Names, 1851–1916

Home Office
HO 10 Convicts, New South Wales and Tasmania, 1788–1859
HO 11 Convict Transportation Registers, 1787–1870
HO 26 Criminal Registers, 1791–1849
HO 27 Criminal Registers, 1805–1892

Ministry of Health
MH 12 Poor Law Union Papers, 1833–1909

Ministry of Transport
MT 23 Admiralty Transport Department, Correspondence and Papers,
          1795–1917

National Debt Office
NDO 4   West Indies Slave Compensation, 1835–1842

Privy Council Office
PC 1   Papers, 1481–1946
PC 2   Registers, 1540–1960
PC 5   Plantation Books, 1678–1806

Treasury
T 1   Treasury Board Papers, 1557–1920
T 27   Out Letters, General, 1668–1920
T 29   Minute Books, 1667–1870
T 47   Registers, Various (includes registers of emigrants, 1773–1776,
       T 47/9–12)
T 50   Documents relating to Refugees, 1780–1856
T 52   King's Warrants, 1667–1857
T 53   Warrants relating to Money, 1676–1859
T 54   Warrants not relating to Money, 1667–1849
T 60   Order Books, 1667–1831
T 71   Slave Registration and Compensation, 1812–1846
T 77   East Florida Claims Commission, 1740–1789
T 79   American Loyalist Claims Commission, 1777–1841
T 99   Minute Books, Supplementary, 1690–1691, 1830–1832

Treasury Solicitor's Office
TS 12   West New Jersey Society, 1658–1921

War Office
WO 1   In-Letters, 1732–1869 (for emigration of Army pensioners, 1846–1851)
WO 43   Old Series Papers, 1809–1857 (for papers on emigration of poor
        pensioners)

18 Clergymen

There are several published works, in particular *Crockford's* and the lists of
Oxford and Cambridge *Alumni,* which you should first consult for
information about Anglican clergy. Records relating to ordinations will be
found in the appropriate diocesan archive and there is a card index of clergy
in the library of the Society of Genealogists (the Fawcett Index). In the
nineteenth century there were insurance companies which dealt exclusively
with clergy life policies. The records of London companies, held in Guildhall
library, may provide a wealth of personal details.

The PRO has Clergy Institution Books (E 331), indexed by the name of the
incumbent, for the period 1556–1838, which give the name of the clergyman,
his parish, his patron and the date. The Ecclesiastical Census of 1851 might
be worth consulting (HO 129).

Bibliography

Publishing Finding Aids

Crockford's Clerical Directory (Oxford, from 1858)

J Foster, *Alumni Oxonienses, 1500-1886* (Oxford, 1891)
J Le Neve, *Fasti Ecclesie Anglicanae* (London, 1716)
J and J A Venn, *Alumni Cantabrigienses, from the Earliest Times to 1900*
    (Cambridge, 1922-1927)

Unpublished Finding Aids

Institution Books, Indexes, 1556-1838, MS
The Ecclesiastical Census of 1851, PRO leaflet no. 3

Records

Exchequer
E 331   Bishops' Certificates of Institution to Benefices, 1544-1912

Home Office
HO 129   Census Papers: Ecclesiastical Returns, 1851

19 Lawyers

From 1775 onwards the easiest means of reference to lawyers is the *Law List*,
published every year. Apart from this, for barristers, many of the records of
the various Inns of Court have been printed, and the lists of *Alumni* of
Oxford and Cambridge should be useful. For attorneys and solicitors
practising between 1730 and 1775, you can use the articles of clerkship in the
PRO. There is no central index or system for these: the articles of an attorney
are found among the records of the court where he was admitted to practise.

For civilian lawyers, i.e. those who practised in the church courts and the
High Court of Admiralty, there is a selective card index of advocates and
proctors in the PRO. The admission of London proctors (attorneys), namely
those practising in Doctor's Commons, was recorded in the Registers of the
Archbishop of Canterbury, kept at Lambeth Palace Library. There are short
biographies of the London advocates (civilian barristers) in the work by G D
Squibb. Records of lawyers who practised in provincial church courts are
probably best sought in diocesan and county record offices.

As in the case of the clergy some nineteenth century insurance companies
specialised in lawyers' life policies. Records relating to London companies are
in the Guildhall Library.

Bibliography

Published Finding Aids

Act Books of the Archbishops of Canterbury, 1663-1859, 2 parts ed, E H W
    Dunkin, C Jenkins and E A Fry (British Record Society, Index Library, 1929)
Law List (annually from 1775)
List of Attorneys and Solicitors admitted in pursuance of the late Act 1729-1731
    (London, 1729-1731)
G D Squibb, *Doctors' Commons* (Oxford, 1977)

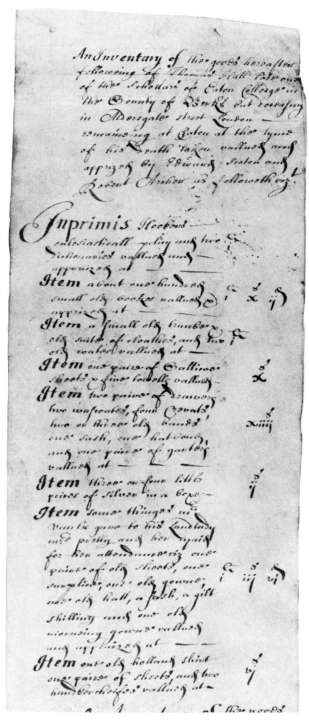

**VI Part of the inventory of the possessions of
Thomas Hall, an Eton schoolboy, 11 Oct. 1676**
(PROB 4/10015)

**VII Sketches of searchers for wills in the
Prerogative Office in Doctors' Commons.
Nineteenth century** (PROB 45)

Card index to advocates and proctors (available on request)
Records of Attorneys and Solicitors (TS, search rooms)

Records

Chancery
C 217   Petty Bag Office, Miscellaneous Papers, Elizabeth I to 1889

Palatinate of Chester
CHES 36   Attorneys, 1697–1830

Court of Common Pleas
CP 5   Articles of Clerkship, 1730–1838
CP 8   Admission Rolls, 1838–1860
CP 10   Oath Rolls, 1779–1847
CP 11   Rolls of Attorneys, 1730–1750

Palatinate of Durham
DURH 3   Cursitor's Records, 1311–1865 (for Oath Roll of Attorneys,
         1730–1841 and File of Admissions of Attorneys, 1660–1723,
         DURH 3/217–218)
DURH 9   Affidavits of Attorneys' Clerks, 1750–1834

Exchequer of Pleas
E 3   Attorneys' Oath Rolls, 1830–1872
E 4   Books of Attorneys, 1830–1855

Exchequer: King's Remembrancer
E 108   Solicitors' Certificate Book, 1785–1843
E 200   Solicitors' Oath Roll, 1772–1841

Supreme Court of Judicature
J 8   Articles of Clerkship, 1876–1904
J 9   Affidavits of due execution of Articles of Clerkship, 1875–1903

Court of King's Bench
KB 104   Articles of Clerkship, 1838–1875
KB 105   Affidavits of due execution of Articles of Clerkship, 1775–1817
KB 106   Affidavits of due execution of Articles of Clerkship, 1817–1834
KB 107   Affidavits of due execution of Articles of Clerkship, 1834–1875

Palatinate of Lancaster
PL 23   Articles of Clerkship, 1730–1875

20 Bankrupts

Insolvents who went through the legal procedure of declaring themselves
bankrupt can be found in the *London Gazette*. There are bankruptcy registers
of petitions from 1912 in the Thomas More Buildings of the Royal Courts of
Justice, in which you can have a brief search made for a fee. The PRO holds
records of bankruptcy proceedings (B) for the period 1710–1958, but they are
closed for 75 years.

Bibliography

Published Finding Aids

London Gazette (annually from 1665, originally called the *Oxford Gazette*)

Records

Court of Bankruptcy
B 3   Bankruptcy Commissions Files, 1759–1911
B 9   Proceedings under the Bankruptcy Acts, from 1832 (subject to 75 year closure)

Board of Trade
BT 40/25–52   Registers of Bankruptcies in London (1870–1886) and County Courts (1870–1884)

21 Criminals

There is a vast mass of documentation on crime in the PRO but the records are not easy to handle and the genealogist should be prepared for a long and possibly unrewarding task. It has frequently been found that newspaper reports of crimes give considerably more detail than can be found in surviving court records.

For petty larceny and breaches of the peace the best place to start looking is in the county record office, among the quarter sessions records, many of which are in print. Minor offences could also be dealt with by the manorial court (see V below).

Of the material in the PRO, the assize records (ASSI) usually provide little genealogical information, except the accused's place of residence, which you will find in the indictment. If depositions happen to survive the names, ages and addresses of the deponents will be given. Unless your period and area are covered by the published calenders, a speculative search is ill advised. The records of the Central Criminal Court at the Old Bailey (which was also the Assize Court for London from 1834) are in the process of being transferred to the PRO (CRIM). More recent records are retained by the court. There are printed copies of proceedings from 1801 to 1904 (PCOM 1); the Home Office records contain returns made by the Clerk of the Sessions of prisoners committed for trial at the Old Bailey from 1815 to 1849 (HO 16). The records of London sessions for gaol delivery and oyer and terminer before 1834 are in the Corporation of London Record Office; those for Middlesex are in the Greater London Record Office. You may also find the registers and calendars of prisons helpful, and relatively easy to use (HO 26, HO 27, HO 77, HO 140, MEPO 6).

For prisoners deported to the colonies see IV/17 above.

Bibliography

Published Finding Aids

Calendar of Assize Records, Hertfordshire Indictments, Elizabeth I and *James I*, ed. J S Cockburn (London, 1975)

Calendar of Assize Records, Sussex Indictments, Elizabeth I and *James I,* ed.
  J S Cockburn (London, 1975)
Calendar of Assize Records, Essex Indictments, Elizabeth I and *James I* ed.
  J S Cockburn (London, 1978, 1982)
Calendar of Assize Records, Kent Indictments, Elizabeth I, and *James I,* ed.
  J S Cockburn (London, 1979, 1980).
Calendar of Assize Records, Surrey Indictments, Elizabeth I and *James I,* ed.
  J S Cockburn (London, 1980, 1982)

Unpublished Finding Aids

Records of the Clerks of Assize, PRO leaflet No. 29

Records (selection)

ASSI   Clerks of Assize

Central Criminal Court
CRIM 1   Depositions, 1839-1922 (All major crimes; samples only of minor
         crimes)
CRIM 2   Calendar of Depositions, 1923-1930
CRIM 3   Commissions of Oyer and Terminer and Gaol Delivery, 1834-1972
CRIM 4   Indictments, 1834-1841
CRIM 5   Calendars of Indictments, 1833-1844
CRIM 6   Courts Books, 1834-1949
CRIM 8   Central Criminal Court Miscellaneous Books and Papers, 1824-1968

DPP   Director of Public Prosecutions, 1846-1952 (closed for 75 years)

Home Office
HO 16   Old Bailey Sessions, 1815-1849
HO 26   Criminal Registers, 1791-1840
HO 27   Criminal Registers, 1805-1892
HO 77   Newgate Calendar, 1782-1853
HO 140   Calendars of Prisoners, 1868-1958

KB   Court of King's Bench

Metropolitan Police
MEPO 6   Habitual Criminals Registers, 1881-1941 (closed for 75 years)

Prison Commission
PCOM 1   Sessions Papers, Old Bailey, 1801-1904
PCOM 2   Prisons Records Series I, 1770-1916 (closed for 100 years)
PCOM 5   Old Captions and Transfer Papers, 1843-1871
PRIS   King's Bench, Fleet and Marshalsea Prisons, 1685-1862

22 Victims of Civil Air Crashes

Records

Ministry of Aviation
AVIA 5 Aircraft Accident Reports, 1919-1936 (for names of pilots, owners
       and passengers)

23 Railwaymen

The records of the railway companies and their staffs before nationalisation are now in the PRO (RAIL). The volume of documentation, however, varies considerably from one company to another.

Unpublished Finding Aids

Card index of subjects to British Transport Historical Records

Records

RAIL   British Transport Historical Records

24 Prisoners of War

Most records in the PRO on prisoners of war from before the two World Wars relate to the expenses of holding foreign prisoners. The exception is a collection of returns of British prisoners at Lille in 1798 (WO 28).

For the South African War (1899-1902) there are lists of Boer prisoners among the records of the War Office (WO 108/302-5).

No lists of First World War prisoners (on either side) ever reached the PRO.

For the Second World War there are no nominal lists of prisoners in British hands. For British prisoners you can apply first to the Ministry of Defence and then to the International Committee of the Red Cross who hold lists of prisoners from both World Wars. Narratives of individual escapees are in the PRO, but they are subject to a 75 year closure period (WO 165/39, WO 208/3242-3566). Report of Red Cross inspections of prison camps (WO 222, WO 224) are available as is material gleaned from contact with prisoners by radio or from escapees (WO 165).

Information about RAF prisoners may be sought in the AIR classes listed below. Particularly useful is a list of air force prisoners in German hands, 1944-45 (AIR 20/2336).

For Prisoners of War at Verdun between 1804 and 1815, there is in France an index of births, marriages and deaths, which can be searched for you for a fee, by Mme M Audin, to whom you should write.

Bibliography

Unpublished Finding Aids

Prisoners of War, PRO leaflet no. 39

Air Ministry
AIR 2   Air Departments Correspondence, (Code B89), 1887–1980
AIR 20   Unregistered Papers, 1909–1973
AIR 40   Directorate of Intelligence, 1923–1958 (prisoners of war, 1897–1911,
         AIR 40/1544–1552)

Colonial Office
CO 693   Dominions, War of 1914–1918, Prisoners, Original Correspondence,
         1917–1919
CO 754   War of 1914–1918, Prisoners, Register of Correspondence, 1914–1919
CO 755   War of 1914–1918, Prisoners, Register of Out-Letters, 1917–1919

Foreign Office
FO 383   General Correspondence, Prisoners, 1915–1919
FO 916   Consular (War) Department, Prisoners of War and Internees,
         1940–1946

War Office
WO 28   Headquarters, 1746–1901
WO 108   South African War Papers, 1899–1905
WO 165   War Diaries, Directorates, 1938–1947 (MI 9, WO 165/39; MI 19,
         WO 165/41)
WO 208   Directorate of Military Intelligence, 1926–1946
WO 222   Medical Historian, 1914–1949
WO 224   Enemy Prisoner of War Camps, Reports of International Red Cross
         and Protecting Powers, 1941–1947

25 Living Persons

Under very special circumstances, the Red Cross and the Salvation Army will
undertake to trace close relatives, but this is usually only to mitigate suffering.
The Association of Genealogists and Record Agents will supply the name of
an agent who will make a search for a fee. Tracing may also be carried out
through the Department of Health and Social Security. You should obtain
leaflet PAS.6 from the General Register Office.

26 Metropolitan Police

Certificates of service for members of the Metropolitan Police for the period
1889–1909, and registers of joiners and leavers for 1829–1947 are in the PRO.
For men serving in the provinces application should be made to the
appropriate local force.

Bibliography

MEPO 4   Office of the Commissioner: Miscellaneous Books and Papers
         1818–1979 (Index available).

V Pre-parish register genealogy

Before the introduction of parish registers in the middle of the sixteenth century, most people's lives went undocumented. Such records as exist are largely the random survivals of private transactions and the records of litigation and of the sovereign's interference with his subjects. Because of the difficulties of reading and searching medieval records, the genealogist is advised to steer clear of anything that does not have some modern means of reference. It would be senseless for you to plunge into the Plea Rolls of the Court of Common Pleas, for instance.

The standard stock-in-trade of the medieval genealogist are Inquisitions Post Mortem (I.P.M.s), Feet of Fines, the Rolls of various courts and wills. Inquisitions (C 132–C 143, C 145, E 136, E 149–E 152) were inquests concerning the estates of tenants in chief (i.e. tenants holding directly from the Crown) on their death. There are a number of calendars in print, and many also have been published by local record societies. The Feet of Fines (CP 25, DURH 12) are the records of fictitious law suits entered into so as to evade conveyancing restrictions, and they run from 1190 until 1833. Many of these, too, have been printed by local record societies. The indexes to Feet of Fines in the Court of Common Pleas are listed in the *Catalogue of Lists and Indexes, KB and CP*.

The best place to look for ordinary, humble folk is on the court roll of the appropriate manor. This gives details of minor offences, and of land held by copyhold from the lord of the manor. You may also find some pedigrees. There are a number of manorial court rolls in the PRO (see the published list), but most are elsewhere, and you should consult the National Register of Archives at the Historical Manuscripts Commission to locate them. For land held freehold there are many thousands of deeds in the PRO, but no central index, so the one in the *Calendar of Ancient Deeds* is valuable (C 146–C 148; see III/7 above).

Medieval genealogy in the PRO is largely a question of looking through the indexes to the various calendars of the rolls of Chancery, Exchequer and King's Bench. The Charter Rolls (C 53), for example, contain grants of land and privileges; the Patent Rolls (C 66) have grants for life, commissions and licences to alienate land; and the back of the Close Rolls (C 54, C 55) were used to enroll all kinds of private deeds, including those for sales, leases, enclosure awards, bankrupts' estates, change of name and naturalisation. There are many pedigrees on the Curia Regis (KB 26) and the Plea Rolls (CP 40). You may also find useful the copious extracts, mainly from the De Banco

(Plea) Rolls and similar legal records, made by General Plantagenet-Harrison in the late nineteenth century. There are several volumes, all hand-written with indexes, which are on the whole reliable. His main interests were in Yorkshire, and in all pedigrees, but you should be cautious in trusting to the accuracy of the latter.

Tax returns can also be useful, the list of Subsidy Rolls (E 179) indicates where names appear. The Certificates of Residence (E 115) give the names and addresses of many sixteenth and seventeenth century tax payers with a valuation of their property; they were returned by people who were not permanently resident in one place, many because they had two or more homes, so as to avoid being assessed twice.

See also III/3, 6, 7 and 8 above.

Bibliography

Books

M W Beresford, 'Lay Subsidies', I '1290-1334'; II 'after 1334', *Amateur Historian,* vol. III (1958), pp. 325-328, vol. IV (1959), pp. 101-109

M W Beresford, 'Poll Taxes of 1377, 1379 and 1381', *Amateur Historian,* vol. III (1958), pp. 271-278

R F Hunnisett, "The Reliability of Inquisitions as Historical Evidence', *The Study of Medieval Records,* ed. D A Bullough and R L Storey (Oxford, 1971)

R E Latham, 'Hints on Interpreting the Public Records, III Inquisitions Post Mortem'; 'IV Plea Rolls', *Amateur Historian,* vol. I (1953), pp. 77-81, 155-158

M McGuiness, 'Inquisitions Post Mortem', *Amateur Historian,* vol. VI, no. 7 (1965), pp. 235-242

Published Finding Aids

British National Archives, Government Publications, Sectional List 24 (revised annually)

Calendar of Charter Rolls, 1226-1516 (London, 1903-1927)

Calendar of Close Rolls, 1227-1509 (London, 1892-1963)

Calendar of Fine Rolls, 1272-1509 (London, 1911-1963)

Calendar of Inquisitions Miscellaneous, Henry III to Henry VII (London, 1916-1969)

Calendar of Inquisitions Post Mortem, Henry III to Henry VII (London, 1898-1974)

Calendar of Patent Rolls, 1216-1578 (London, 1891-1982)

'Calendarium Genealogicum: or Calendar of Heirs, extracted from the Inquisitions, temp. Edward II, 1-2 Edward II,' *Deputy Keeper's Report,* XXXII (1871), appendix 1, pp. 237-263; 3-4 Edward II, ed. J A C Vincent, *The Genealogist,* n.s. vols. 1-4, 6 (1884-1887, 1889)

Calendarium Genealogicum, Henry III and Edward I, ed. C Roberts (London, 1865)

Calendarium . . . Inquisitionum ad quod Damnum, 1 Edward II to 38 Henry VI, ed. J Caley and R Lemon (London, 1803)

Calendarium Inquisitionum Post Mortem sive Escaetarum, ed. J Caley and J Bayley (London, 1806–1828)

Curia Regis Rolls, Richard I–26 Henry III (London, 1923–1979)

Descriptive Catalogue of Ancient Deeds, from before James I (London, 1890–1915)

Index of Inquisitions Post Mortem, Henry VIII to Charles, I, PRO Lists and Indexes, vols. XXIII, XXVI, XXXI and XXXIII (London, 1907–1909)

Index of Persons named in Early Chancery Proceedings, 1385–1467, ed. C A Walmisley (Harleian Society, London, 1927–1928)

List and Index of Court Rolls, PRO Lists and Indexes, vol. VI, pt 1 (London, 1896)

'Inquisitiones post mortem temp Henry VIII to Charles I,' *The Genealogist,* n.s. vols. 9–19 (1893–1903), 25–34 (1908–1920)

Rotuli Curiae Regis, 6 Richard I–1 John, ed. F Palgrave (London, 1835)

G Wrottesley, *Pedigrees from the Plea Rolls, 1200–1500* (London, c. 1906)

Unpublished Finding Aids

PRO card index of records in print
List of Exchequer KR Subsidy Rolls, Law Series (1925), TS
Index of names in Certificates of Residence, Edward VI–Charles II, TS
Plantagenet-Harrison notes from legal records, MS
Catalogue of Lists and Indexes, KB and CP, TS

Records

Chancery
C 53   Charter Rolls, 1 John to 8 Henry VIII
C 54   Close Rolls, 6 John to 1903
C 55   Close Rolls, Supplementary, 27 Henry III to 12 Henry VI
C 60   Fine Rolls, 1 John to 23 Charles I
C 66   Patent Rolls, 3 John to 9 George VI
C 132   Inquisitions Post Mortem: Henry III
C 133   Inquisitions Post Mortem: Edward I
C 134   Inquisitions Post Mortem: Edward II
C 135   Inquisitions Post Mortem: Edward III
C 136   Inquisitions Post Mortem: Richard II
C 137   Inquisitions Post Mortem: Henry IV
C 138   Inquisitions Post Mortem: Henry V
C 139   Inquisitions Post Mortem: Henry VI
C 140   Inquisitions Post Mortem: Edward IV
C 141   Inquisitions Post Mortem: Richard III
C 142   Inquisitions Post Mortem: Henry VII to Charles II
C 143   Inquisitions ad quod damnum, Henry III to Richard III
C 145   Inquisitions, Miscellaneous, 3 Henry III to 2 Richard III
C 146   Ancient Deeds, Series C, before 1603
C 147   Ancient Deeds, Series CC, before 1603
C 148   Ancient Deeds, Series CS, before 1603

Court of Common Pleas
CP 25   Feet of Fines, Henry II to 2 Victoria
CP 40   Plea Rolls, 1 Edward I to 38 Victoria

Palatinate of Durham
DURH 12   Feet of Fines, 1535–1834

Exchequer
E 115   Certificates of Residence, Edward VI to Charles II
E 136   Escheators' Accounts, Henry III to James I
E 149   Inquisitions Post Mortem, Henry III to Richard III
E 150   Inquisitions Post Mortem, Henry VII to James I
E 151   Inquisitions ad quod damnum, Henry III to Henry VI
E 152   Enrolments of Inquisitions, Edward I to Henry VIII
E 179   Subsidy Rolls, c. Henry II to William and Mary

Court of King's Bench
KB 26   Plea (Curia Regis) Rolls, 5 Richard I to 56 Henry III

VI Sources of help

The PRO does not undertake genealogical research, but in some cases will do brief searches for specific items, if supplied with sufficient information. If you wish someone to do a full search on your behalf a list of agents may be supplied but, the arrangement between yourself and the agent will be of a purely private nature. The Association of Genealogists and Record Agents will also put you in touch with an accredited researcher. If you have sound reasons for believing that your family is 'armigerous' (entitled to bear a coat of arms) you should enquire of the Officer-in-Waiting at the College of Arms.

There is a network of family history societies throughout the British Isles, most of which publish journals. These organisations can be extremely helpful in providing professional guidance and contact between family historians. A list of family history societies and like bodies is published in the journal of the Federation of Family History Societies, the *Family History News and Digest,* published quarterly.

The Society of Genealogists has a genealogical library and a number of very useful indexes. It is open to members and to anyone else on a daily fee-paying basis. The Guildhall Library in London is a public library with an excellent genealogical collection.

The Historical Manuscripts Commission will provide information about the whereabouts of private papers.

VII Useful addresses

Alberta Genealogical Society
  Box 21015
  Edmonton T5J 3L2
  Canada

Anglo-Jewish Archives
  The Mocatta Library
  University College
  Gower Street
  London WC1E 6BT

Army Medal Office
  Government Office Buildings
  Droitwich
  Worcs WR9 8AU

Army Museums Ogilby Trust
  Connaught Barracks
  Duke of Connaught's Road
  Aldershot
  Hants GU11 2LR

Association of Genealogists and Record
Agents
  Honorary Secretary
  64 Oakleigh Park North
  London N20 9AS

Association of Scottish Genealogists
and Record Agents
  Secretary Sheila Pitcairn, LGH,
  FSA, Scot.
  106 Brucefield Avenue
  Dunfermline KY11 4SY

Audin, Mme M.
  37 Rue La Quintinie
  75015 Paris
  France

Australian Genealogists, Society of
  Richmond Villa
  120 Kent Street
  Observatory Hill
  Sydney NSW 2000

Baptist Historical Society
  Baptist Union Library
  4 Southampton Row
  London WC1B 4AB

British Information Services
  845 Third Avenue
  New York
  NY 0022
  U.S.A.

British Columbia Genealogical Society
  Box 94371
  Richmond
  British Columbia V6Y 2A8
  Canada

British Library, Reference Division
  Great Russell Street
  London WC1B 3DG

British Red Cross Society
  International Welfare Department
  9 Grosvenor Crescent
  London SW1X 7EJ

Cabinet Office
  Management and Personnel Office
  Alencon Links
  Basingstoke RG21 1JB

Canterbury Cathedral Archives and
Library
  The Precincts
  Canterbury CT1 2EG

Mr Hilary Carré
  Registrar
  La Vallette
  Sark, C.I.

Catholic Central Library
  47 Francis Street
  London SW1P QR

Catholic Record Society
  c/o Miss R Rendel
  114 Mount Street
  London W1Y 6AH

Central Bureau voor Genealogie
  Prins Willem-Alexander-hof 22
  2595 BE DEN HAAG
  The Netherlands
Mailing address:
  P.O. Box 11755
  2502 AT DEN HAAG
  The Netherlands

Central Criminal Court
  Courts' Administrator
  Old Bailey
  London EC4M 7EH

Channel Islands Family History Society
  c/o Mrs M L Backhurst
  "Le Jardin"
  Rue de Francheville
  Grouville
  Jersey, C.I.

Chaplain of the Fleet
  Ministry of Defence
  Lacon House
  Theobalds Road
  London WC1X 8RY

Church of Jesus Christ of the Latter
Day Saints
  Hyde Park Chapel
  64 Exhibition Road
  London SW7 2PA

Clerk of the Court
  Queen Elizabeth II Street
  Alderney, C.I.

College of Arms
  Queen Victoria Street
  London EC4V 4BT

Companies Registration Office
  London Search Room
  Companies House
  55-71 City Road
  London EC1Y 1BB

Companies Registration Office
  Crown Way
  Maindy
  Cardiff CF4 3UZ

Commonwealth War Graves
Commission
  2 Marlow Road
  Maidenhead
  Berks SL6 7DX

Corporation of London Record
Office
  Guildhall
  London EC2P 2EJ

Defence, Ministry of
CS (R) 2a   (Royal Navy Medals)
CS (R) 2b   (Army Personnel Records)
CS (R) 2c   (Polish Service Personnel
Records)
CS (R) 2e   (Naval Personnel Records)
  Bourne Avenue
  Hayes
  Middx UBC 1RS

Department of Health and Social
Security
  Scholfield Mills
  Brunswick Street
  Nelson
  Lancs BB9 0HU

District Probate Registries
  Cavendish House
  Waterloo Street
  Birmingham B2 2NA

28 Richmond Place
Brighton BN2 2NA

Ground Floor
The Crescent Centre
Temple Back
Bristol BS 6EP

17–19 Cornhill
Ipswich IP1 1DF

Devereux House
East Parade
Leeds LS1 2BA

The English Catholic Ancestor
c/o Leslie Brooks
Hill House West
Crookham Village
Aldershot
Hants GU13 O55

The Family History Association of
Canada
PO Box 398
West Vancouver
British Columbia V7V 3P1
Canada

Federation of Family History Societies
General Secretary
96 Beaumont Street
Mile House
Plymouth PL2 3AQ

French Research Organisation for
Genealogical Services
37 Rue La Quintinie
75015 Paris
France

Genealogical Office
National Library
Kildare Street
Dublin 2

Genealogical Society of South Africa
15 Queens Road
Tanboerskloof
Capetown
South Africa 8001

Genealogical Society of Utah
50 East North Temple
Salt Lake City
Utah 84150
U.S.A.

General Register Office (CA Section)
Titchfield
Fareham
Hants PO15 5RR

General Register Office
Office of Population Censuses and
Surveys
St Catherine's House
10 Kingsway
London WC2B 6JP
(births and marriages)
and
Alexandra House
Kingsway WC2
(deaths only; all correspondence to be
directed to St Catherine's House)

General Registry
Finch Road
Douglas
Isle of Man

Greater London Record Office
40 Northampton Road
London EC1R 0HB

HM Greffier
The Greffe
Royal Court House
St Peter Port
Guernsey, C.I.

Guildhall Library
Aldermanbury
London EC2P 2EJ

D Harrington
143 Sturry Road
Canterbury
Kent CT1 1DF

Historical Manuscripts Commission
Quality House
Quality Court
Chancery Lane
London WC2A 1HF

Home Office
Lunar House
Wellesley Road
Croydon CR9 2BY

The Honourable Society of
Cymmrodorion
30 Eastcastle Street
London W1N 7PD

Huguenot Library
University College
Gower Street
London WC1E 6BT

Huguenot Society
Miss I Scouloudi, Honorary
Secretary
67 Victoria Road
London W8 5RH
(postal enquiries only)

Huguenot Society of Germany
Deutsche Hugenotten-Verein e. V.
Geschäftstelle
Postfach 35
D 3305 SICKTE
W Germany

Imperial War Museum
Lambeth Road
London SE1 6HZ

India Office Library and Records
Foreign and Commonwealth Office
197 Blackfriars Road
London SE1 8NG

Institute of Heraldic and Genealogical
Studies
Northgate
Canterbury
Kent CT1 1BA

The Archivist
International Red Cross
British Red Cross Training Centre
Barnett Hill
Wonersh
Guildford
Surrey GU5 3PJ

Irish Genealogical Research Society
c/o F B Payton
Glenholme
High Oatham Road
Mansfield
Nottingham

Jewish Museum
Woburn House
Upper Woburn Place
London WC1H 0EP

John Rylands University Library
Oxford Road
Manchester M13 9PP

Lambeth Palace Library
London SE1 7JU

HM Land Registry
Lincoln's Inn Fields
London WC2A 3PH

Manx Museum Library
Kingswood Grove
Douglas
Isle of Man

Maritime History Group
Memorial University of
Newfoundland
St John's
Newfoundland
Canada

Methodist Connection Archivists
c/o The Property Division
Central Hall
Oldham Street
Manchester M1 1JQ

National Army Museum
Royal Hospital Road
London SW3 4HT

National Genealogical Society
1921 Sunderland Place N W.
Washington D.C. 20036
U.S.A.

National Library of Wales
Aberystwyth SY23 3BU

National Maritime Museum
Greenwich
London SE10 9NF

New Zealand Society of Genealogists
PO Box 8795
Symonds Street
Auckland
New Zealand

Norfolk Record Office
Central Library
Norwich NR2 1NJ

Ontario Genealogical Society
Box 66
Stn. Q
Toronto M4T 2L7
Canada

Presbyterian Historical Society of
Northern Ireland
Church House
Fisherwick Place
Belfast BT1 6DU

The Priaulx Library
St Peter Port
Guernsey, C.I.

Principal Registry of the Family
Division
Somerset House
Strand
London WC2R 1LA

Public Archives of Canada
395 Wellington Street
Ottawa 4
Ontario K1A 0NA

Public Record Office of Ireland
Custom House
Dublin

Registrar General of Northern Ireland
49–55 Chichester Street
Belfast BT1 4HL

Registrar General of Scotland
New Register House
Princess Street
Edinburgh EH1 3YT

Registrar General of Shipping and
Seamen
Llantrisant Road
Llandaff
Cardiff CF5 2YS

Registrar of Companies
102 George Street
Edinburgh EH2 3DJ

Registrar of the Ecclesiastical Court
12 New Street
St Peter Port
Guernsey, C.I.

Registry of Deeds
Henrietta Street
Dublin

Religious Society of Friends
The Librarian
Friends' House
Euston House
London NW1 2BJ

RAF Personnel Management Centre
Eastern Avenue
Barnwood
Gloucester GL4 7AN

Royal Archives
Windsor Castle
Windsor
Berks SL4 1NJ

Royal Courts of Justice
  Strand
  London WC2A 2LL

Royal Artillery Manning and Record
Office
  Imphal Barracks
  York YO1 4HD

Royal Marines' Drafting and Record
Office
  HMS *Centurion*
  Grange Road
  Portsmouth PO13 9XA

RN Medals OS10
  Empress State Building
  Lillie Road
  London SW6 1TR

Salvation Army
  (The Investigating Officer)
  110–112 Middlesex Street
  London E1 7HY

Scottish Genealogical Society
  c/o Miss J Ferguson
  21 Howard Place
  Edinburgh EH3 5JY

Scottish Record Office
  PO Box 36
  HM General Register House
  Edinburgh EH1 3YY

Scottish Tartan Society
  Davidson House
  Drummond Street
  Comrie
  Crieff
  Perthshire

Scots Ancestral Research Society
  3 Albany Street
  Edinburgh EH1 3PY

Society of Genealogists
  14 Charterhouse Buildings
  London EC1M 7AN

Société Jersiaise
  The Museum
  Pier Road
  St Helier
  Jersey, C.I.

Southampton City Record Office
  Civic Centre
  Southampton SO9 4XR

Spanish and Portuguese Synagogue
  9 Lauderdale Road
  Maida Vale
  London W9 1LT

Mrs E R Stage
  150 Fulwell Park Avenue
  Twickenham
  Middx TW2 5HB

Superintendent of Births, Marriages
and Deaths
  The States Building
  Royal Square
  St Helier
  Jersey, C.I.

United Reformed Church History
Society
  86 Tavistock Place
  London WC1H 9RT

United Synagogue, Offices of the
  Woburn House
  Upper Woburn Place
  London WC1H 0EZ

Dr Williams's Library
  14 Gordon Square
  London WC1H 0AG

Women's Land Army Benevolent
Association
  c/o Mrs Lovegrove
  Room 216
  Eagle House
  90–96 Cannon Street
  London EC4

Appendix
How to find a record of a birth or baptism

i   Read the FIRST question

ii   Answer 'yes' or 'no' to it, and then read the item to which you are referred.

iii   Carry on in this way reading ONLY the items you are instructed to read.

iv   Some items are instructions for searching. If the search is unsuccessful continue with the items to which you are referred.

1	Was the birth in England or Wales?	YES NO	*read* 28 *read* 2
2	Was the birth in Scotland?	YES NO	*read* 3 *read* 4
3	Consult records in General Registry, Edinburgh	UNSUCCESSFUL	*read* 85
4	Was the birth in Ireland?	YES NO	*read* 5 *read* 10
5	Was the birth before 1 January 1922?	YES NO	*read* 8 *read* 6
6	Was the birth in Southern Ireland?	YES NO	*read* 9 *read* 7
7	Consult General Register Office, Belfast.	UNSUCCESSFUL	*read* 85
8	Was the birth after 1864?	YES NO	*read* 9 *read* 85
9	Consult General Register Office, Dublin.	UNSUCCESSFUL	*read* 85
10	Was the birth in India, Burma, Aden, St Helena, South-East Asia?	YES NO	*read* 11 *read* 12
11	Consult India Office Records.	UNSUCCESSFUL	*read* 13
12	Was the birth elsewhere in the Commonwealth?	YES NO	*read* 13 *read* 14
13	Consult registers in country of birth. See: General Register Office, *Abstract of arrangements respecting registration of births, marriages and deaths in the United Kingdom and the other countries of the British Commonwealth . . .* (London, 1952).	UNSUCCESSFUL	*read* 19

14	Was the birth elsewhere abroad?	YES	*read 15*
		NO	*read 22*
15	Were the parents British?	YES	*read 17*
		NO	*read 16*
16	Consult immigration records in the Public Record Office.	UNSUCCESSFUL	*read 85*
17	Was the birth in St Petersburg, Russia, 1818–1840?	YES	*read 18*
		NO	*read 19*
18	Search RG 4/4605 in the Public Record Office.	UNSUCCESSFUL	*read 19*
19	Consult registers of births overseas, RG 32–36 in the Public Record Office and 'foreign' section at St. Catherine's House.	UNSUCCESSFUL	*read 20*
20	Consult Bishop of London's Registers at Guildhall Library, London.	UNSUCCESSFUL	*read 21*
21	Consult miscellaneous registers at Lambeth Palace Library.	UNSUCCESSFUL	*read 85*
22	Was the birth at sea?	YES	*read 23*
		NO	*read 27*
23	Were the parents British?	YES	*read 29*
		NO	*read 24*
24	Was the birth after 1854?	YES	*read 25*
		NO	*read 85*
25	Was the ship British?	YES	*read 26*
		NO	*read 85*
26	Consult records of the Registrar of Shipping and Seamen in the Public Record Office.	UNSUCCESSFUL	*read 85*
27	Was the birth in a British aircraft?	YES	*read 29*
		NO	*read 85*
28	Was the birth before 1 July 1837?	YES	*read 30*
		NO	*read 29*
29	Consult records in General Register Office.	UNSUCCESSFUL	*read 85*
30	Was the birth after 1538?	YES	*read 31*
		NO	*read 85*
31	Is the place of birth known or assumed?	YES	*read 47*
		NO	*read 32*
32	Is the residence in 1841, 1851, 1861 or 1871 known?	YES	*read 33*
		NO	*read 34*
33	Consult census records in the Public Record Office.	UNSUCCESSFUL	*read 34*
34	Did the person serve subsequently in the British Army?	YES	*read 35*
		NO	*read 36*
35	Consult records of military service in the Public Record Office.	UNSUCCESSFUL	*read 36*

36	Did the person serve subsequently in the Royal Navy?	YES NO	*read* 37 *read* 38
37	Consult records of naval service in the Public Record Office.	UNSUCCESSFUL	*read* 38
38	Did the person serve subsequently in the Army, Marine or Civil Service in India or with the East India Company?	YES NO	*read* 39 *read* 40
39	Consult India Office Records.	UNSUCCESSFUL	*read* 40
40	Did the person serve subsequently in the Merchant Navy?	YES NO	*read* 41 *read* 42
41	Consult Records of the Registrar General of Shipping and Seamen in the Public Record Office.	UNSUCCESSFUL	*read* 42
42	Did the person serve subsequently in the British Civil Service?	YES NO	*read* 43 *read* 45
43	Was he appointed after 1855?	YES NO	*read* 44 *read* 45
44	Consult HM Treasury	UNSUCCESSFUL	*read* 45
45	Did the person subsequently emigrate?	YES NO	*read* 46 *read* 85
46	Consult emigration records in the Public Record Office.	UNSUCCESSFUL	*read* 85
47	Is the religious denomination of the person or his parents known?	YES NO	*read* 60 *read* 48
48	Was the person born at the British Lying-in Hospital Holborn?	YES NO	*read* 49 *read* 50
49	Consult RG 8/52–66 in the Public Record Office.	UNSUCCESSFUL	*read* 50
50	Was the person baptised in the Fleet or King's Bench Prisons, Mayfair Chapel or the Mint?	YES NO	*read* 51 *read* 52
51	Consult RG 7 in the Public Record Office.	UNSUCCESSFUL	*read* 84
52	Was the person baptised in Greenwich Hospital?	YES NO	*read* 53 *read* 54
53	Consult RG 4/1669, 1670, 1677, 1678 in the Public Record Office.	UNSUCCESSFUL	*read* 84
54	Was the person baptised in Chelsea Hospital?	YES NO	*read* 55 *read* 56
55	Consult RG 4/4330, 4387 in the Public Record Office.	UNSUCCESSFUL	*read* 84
56	Was the person baptised in one of the Chapels Royal?	YES NO	*read* 57 *read* 58
57	Consult RG 8/110 in the Public Record Office.	UNSUCCESSFUL	*read* 84

58	Was the person baptised in Somerset House Chapel?	YES	*read* 59
		NO	*read* 84
59	Consult RG 8/109 in the Public Record Office.	UNSUCCESSFUL	*read* 84
60	Was the person a member of a Foreign Protestant Church?	YES	*read* 61
		NO	*read* 64
61	Consult RG 4 and RG 8 in the Public Record Office.	UNSUCCESSFUL	*read* 62
62	Consult Foreign Protestant Registers in the Guildhall Library, London.	UNSUCCESSFUL	*read* 63
63	Consult the Huguenot Society	UNSUCCESSFUL	*read* 84
64	Was the person a member of a Russian Orthodox church?	YES	*read* 65
		NO	*read* 66
65	Consult RG 8/111-304 in the Public Record Office.	UNSUCCESSFUL	*read* 84
66	Was the person a Quaker (Religious Society of Friends)?	YES	*read* 67
		NO	*read* 69
67	Consult RG 6 and RG 8 in the Public Record Office.	UNSUCCESSFUL	*read* 68
68	Consult the Religious Society of Friends.	UNSUCCESSFUL	*read* 84
69	Was the person a Methodist or Wesleyan?	YES	*read* 70
		NO	*read* 73
70	Was the person born in or around London?	YES	*read* 71
		NO	*read* 77
71	Was the person born after 1818?	YES	*read* 72
		NO	*read* 77
72	Consult RG 4/4677-4680, RG 5/162-207 in the Public Record Office.	UNSUCCESSFUL	*read* 77
73	Was the person a member of some other protestant nonconformist church?	YES	*read* 74
		NO	*read* 78
74	Was the person born in or around London?	YES	*read* 75
		NO	*read* 77
75	Was the person born after 1742?	YES	*read* 76
		NO	*read* 77
76	Consult RG 4/4658-4676, RG 5/1-161 in the Public Record Office.	UNSUCCESSFUL	*read* 77
77	Consult RG 4 and RG 8 in the Public Record Office.	UNSUCCESSFUL	*read* 84
78	Was the person a Roman Catholic?	YES	*read* 79
		NO	*read* 81
79	Consult RG 4 in the Public Record Office.	UNSUCCESSFUL	*read* 80
80	Consult records of Roman Catholic churches held locally.	UNSUCCESSFUL	*read* 84

81	Was the person Jewish?	YES read 82
		NO read 83
82	Consult Synagogue records preserved locally or the Mormon International Genealogical Index.	UNSUCCESSFUL read 85
83	Was the person a member of the Church of England (Anglican)?	YES read 84
		NO read 85
84	Consult Parish Registers held locally or the Mormon International Genealogical Index	UNSUCCESSFUL read 85
85	Take expert advice: e.g. from your local family history society	

Other Public Record Office Publications

Public Record Office Museum Pamphlets

Fascimiles of documents etc., with introductory notes.

1. The Olive Branch Petition. (ISBN 0 11 440038 5) .
2. Tudor Royal Letters: The Family of Henry VIII (ISBN 0 11 440043 1) . . . .
3. Tudor Royal Letters: Elizabeth I and the Succession. (ISBN 0 11 440047 4) . . . .
4. English Royal Signatures. (ISBN 0 11 440052 0) .
5. Royal Portraits from the Plea Rolls: Henry VIII to Charles II. (ISBN 0 11 440056 3) . . . .
6. Men of Letters. (ISBN 0 11 440060 1) . . .
7. Early Chests in Wood and Iron. (ISBN 0 11 440061 X)
8. American Independence: Events to 1776. (ISBN 0 11 440080 6) . . . .
9. American Independence: The War. (ISBN 0 11 440081 4)
10. Domesday Book. (ISBN 0 11 440106 3) . . .
11. English Royal Marriages: The French marriages of Edward I and Edward II, 1299 and 1307. (ISBN 0 11 440104 7) . . . .
12. Mary Queen of Scots. (ISBN 0 11 440105 5) . .

This is your War (ISBN 0 11 440166 7) . . .

Public Record Office Leaflets

Single copies of the following leaflets, which give information on records of particular types or on particular subjects, are available from the Public Record Office Enquiries Desk at Chancery Lane and the Reference Room at Kew.

Records of Births, Marriages and Deaths . . .
Censuses of Population: Documents in the PRO . .
The Ecclesiastical Census of 1851 . . . . .
Probate Records . . . .
Change of Name . . . .
Immigrants . . . .
Emigrants . . . .
Records of the Registrar General of Shipping and Seaman . . . .
British Military Records as Sources for Biography and Genealogy . . . .
Militia muster Rolls 1522–1640 . . . . .
English Local History: a note for beginners . . .
Inclosure Awards . . . .
Tithe Records in the PRO . . . . . .
Agricultural Statistics: Parish Summaries (MAF 68) .
Designs and Trade Marks: Registers and Representations .
The American Revolution: Documents in the PRO .
The Records of the Foreign Office, 1782–1947 . .
Admiralty Records as sources for Biography and Genealogy . . . .
Domesday Book . . . .
Private Conveyances in the PRO . . . . .
Apprenticeship Records as Sources for Genealogy in the PRO . . . .
Royal Marine Records . . . . . .
Records of the Clerks of Assize (ASSI) . . .
Records of the Royal Irish Constabulary . . .
An Introduction to Chancery Proceedings . . .
Markets and Fairs . . . .
Death Duty Registers . . . . . .
Valuation Office records created under the 1910 Finance Act . . . .
Genealogy from the Public Records . . . .
Dockyard Employees: Documents in the Public Record Office . . . .
Prisoners of War: Documents in the Public Record Office.
Operational Records of the British Army in the Great War, 1914–1919 . . . .
Operational Records of the British Army in the Second World War, 1939–1945 . . . . . .
Operational Records of the Royal Navy in the Great War, 1914–1919 . . . .

Public Record Office Reference Guides

The following guides to the class lists and other means of reference to particular series of records are available in the Reference Room at Kew or in the Round Room at Chancery Lane as appropriate

1a. A Guide to the Admiralty Index and Digest (ADM 12).
1b. A Brief Guide to the Admiralty Index and Digest (ADM 12) . . . .
2. ADM 196: Records of Officers' services . . .
3. T 160–164: Treasury registration system, 1920–1948 .
4. Colonial Office Registers . . . . . .
5. Ministry of Labour: LAB 2 and 7 . . . .
6. Cabinet Records . . . .
7. Foreign Office Correspondence: FO 371 . . .
8. Treasury Board Letters and Papers: T 1 . . .
9a. How to Order a Document by Computer . .
9b. Common Mistakes in Ordering a Document by Computer . . . .
10. Hearth Tax Returns . . . .
11. High Court of Admiralty . . . . . .
12. Domesday Book . . . .
13. Treasury Solicitor Papers: TS 11 . . . .
14. Typical Procedure for the Establishment of a Railway Company . . . .
15. War Diaries: Key to Theatres and Other Headings
16. Home Office Registration . . . . . .
17. How to Find a Will . . . .
18. Searching the Census . . . .
19. Census Photocopies . . . . . .

Public Record Office Handbooks

1. Guide to Seals in the Public Record Office (Second Edition) (ISBN 0 11 440145 4) . . . . .
3. List of Papers of the Committee of Imperial Defence, to 1914. (ISBN 0 11 440147 0). . . . . .
11. The Records of the Cabinet Office to 1922. (ISBN 0 11 440150 0) . . . .
12. The Records of the Forfeited Estates Commission. (ISBN 0 11 440151 9) . . . .
14. Records of Interest to Social Scientists 1919 to 1939: Introduction. (ISBN 0 11 440027 X) . . .
16. Records of Interest to Social Scientists: Unemployment Insurance 1911 to 1939. (ISBN 0 11 440063 6) .
17. The Cabinet Office to 1945. (ISBN 0 11 440034 2).
18. Records of Interest to Social Scientists 1919 to 1939: Employment and Unemployment. (ISBN 0 11 440091 1).
20. The Records of the General Eyre (ISBN 0 11 440123 3).

HER MAJESTY'S STATIONERY OFFICE

Government Bookshops

49 High Holborn, London WC1V 6HB
13a Castle Street, Edinburgh EH2 3AR
Brazennose Street, Manchester M60 8AS
Southey House, Wine Street, Bristol BS1 2BQ
258 Broad Street, Birmingham B1 2HE
80 Chichester Street, Belfast BT1 4JY

*Government publications are also available
through booksellers*

Printed in England for Her Majesty's Stationery Office

Dd 737354 C90 7/84